Step Away From That Sentence

Saoirse Temple

Published by Saoirse Temple, 2025.

While every precaution has been taken in the preparation of this book, the publisher assumes no responsibility for errors or omissions, or for damages resulting from the use of the information contained herein.

STEP AWAY FROM THAT SENTENCE

First edition. October 23, 2025.

Copyright © 2025 Saoirse Temple.

ISBN: 978-1069750594

Written by Saoirse Temple.

Also by Saoirse Temple

Bounders
The Fire of Orhowyn
The Amber Chalice
The Power of Averborn

Dear Diary Style Files
Dear Diary: Punctuation Can't Save the World (But It Did Save Grandma)
Dear Diary: I Have 99 Problems and All of Them Are Numbers
Dear Diary: I Think the Alphabet is Gaslighting Me!
Dear Diary; I've Committed a Capital Offense
Dear Diary; I Don't Think That Word Means What I Think It Means

Standalone
Step Away From That Sentence

Watch for more at https://www.saoirsetemple.com/.

Table of Contents

Back Away From That Sentence 1
The Noun & Pronoun Underground 5
Verbs—Movers, Shakers, and Rule-Breakers 34
Modifiers—Adverbs and Adjectives 69
Connectors: Prepositions & Conjunctions 109
Sentences & Structure (CSI—Syntax) 118
Agreement & Logic (Play Nice) 131
Grammar Gremlins & Other Nightmares 140
Breaking the Rules on Purpose 149
Author's Note 151
Glossary of Terms, Tricks, and Tiny Tyrants 152

For Alison

Back Away From That Sentence

The Scene of the Crime

Every editor has seen it: a sentence staggering across the page, adjectives clinging like cheap jewelry, commas scattered like broken glass. Somewhere in the wreckage, a preposition gasps its last breath while the subject and verb glare at each other across the chaos.

Grammar gets blamed, of course. It always does. Too strict. Too confusing. Too boring.

But grammar isn't the villain—it's the victim. The real culprit is fear. Fear of sounding foolish, of being corrected, of someone in the comments gleefully pointing out that you used *less* instead of *fewer*.

The truth is, grammar was never about showing off. It's about showing meaning. Rules weren't invented to make writers miserable; they evolved to help words cooperate so that ideas don't trip over their own punctuation. When grammar works, you don't notice it—it's the invisible scaffolding holding your thoughts upright.

This book isn't about turning you into a red-pen-wielding zealot. It's about giving you the tools—and yes, the courage—to tame your sentences instead of running from them. You and grammar are about to get reacquainted. Maybe even reconciled.

Rules, Rebels, and the Myth of Perfection

At some point, someone probably told you grammar was carved into stone by the gods of English. Break a rule, and your sentences would burst into flames. End a sentence with a preposition? Eternal shame. Split an infinitive? Straight to literary purgatory.

The truth is, those "rules" were never divine decrees—they were polite society's idea of linguistic table manners, many borrowed from

Latin, a language that doesn't even work like English. (It's a bit like telling a cat it has to bark now because dogs once did it better.)

Good writers learn the rules so they can see through them. Grammar says, *Don't put your elbows on the table.* Style says, *Unless you're leaning in to tell the best story anyone's heard all week.*

The myth of perfection is grammar's biggest PR problem. There's no one right way to write—only clear, intentional, rhythmic ways. That's why a line like *to boldly go where no one has gone before* still gives us chills: it broke a rule and still *worked*. Language isn't just logic; it's music.

So yes, we'll talk about rules in this book—but not so you can obey them like a hall monitor. You're here to learn their logic, to use them with purpose. Grammar isn't a cage; it's a living map. The goal isn't to stay inside the lines—it's to know where they are when you decide to cross them.

> The word "grammar" comes from Greek "grammatike," but in medieval times it meant "magical learning." That's why "grimoire" (book of spells) shares the same root.

Grammar Rehab

Take a breath. You're safe here. No one's going to confiscate your semicolons or make you diagram a sentence while crying softly into your coffee.

If grammar class left you twitching, you're not alone. Most of us were taught grammar as punishment—a list of don'ts dressed up as education. Don't end with a preposition. Don't start with *and*. Don't split infinitives. Don't dangle anything. (We'll un-dangle that soon enough.)

But grammar doesn't need a drill sergeant—it needs a therapist. It's been misunderstood, misquoted, and occasionally weaponized. Grammar rehab is where we learn that rules can be guides, not guards. The goal isn't perfection—it's fluency.

Your writing muscles already have memory; they just need a little physiotherapy. We're going to stretch them, strengthen them, and laugh when they cramp. By the end, you won't just *know* the rules—you'll *feel* them working beneath your sentences, quietly keeping everything upright while you focus on the story.

The red pen is no longer a weapon.

It's a wand.

Your Mission, Should You Choose to Accept It

Grammar doesn't care about your GPA, your publishing credits, or how often you've used *whom* correctly. It just wants to be understood.

This isn't about memorizing lifeless rules—it's about seeing how language works so you can bend it, stretch it, and occasionally snap it on purpose. Grammar isn't a judge with a clipboard. It's a toolbox. And your mission—should you choose to accept it—is to learn how every tool fits in your hand.

We'll take apart sentences, peek under the hood, and see what makes them purr or stall. You'll meet the parts of speech not as abstract categories but as characters in a messy, brilliant cast: the nouns that name things, the verbs that make them move, the adjectives that overdo it, and the conjunctions trying desperately to hold it all together.

You'll learn that commas aren't decoration—they're choreography. That tense isn't just a timeline—it's tone. That the tiniest preposition can shift everything, and the right modifier can turn a sentence from serviceable to unforgettable.

By the end, you'll write with the kind of confidence that comes from understanding *why* the rules exist—and how to break them beautifully.

So sharpen your pencils, polish your curiosity, and keep your hands where I can see 'em.

You're not just learning grammar. You're about to master meaning.

The Noun & Pronoun Underground

They look innocent enough. Just little words minding their business, naming things and pointing at stuff. But don't be fooled—nouns and pronouns are the shady operatives of the sentence world. They hold the keys to meaning, identity, and chaos, depending on how they're handled.

Every sentence needs someone to *do* something and someone or something to *be* that thing. That's where nouns come in: the workhorses, the anchors, the cast list of every linguistic drama. Without them, verbs would be pacing nervously, wondering what exactly they're supposed to move.

But nouns alone can't keep the lights on—that's where pronouns step in, sneaky little shapeshifters designed to make your sentences sound natural and keep you from repeating "the wizard" twenty-seven times in one paragraph. Unfortunately, pronouns are also petty. They demand clarity, agreement, and a very specific kind of attention. One slip, and they'll leave your reader wondering who "she" even is and why "they" just set fire to the metaphorical castle.

This section is where we meet the grammar crew that gives names, faces, and stand-ins to everything else that follows. You'll discover how nouns can be both solid and slippery, how collective ones can spark arguments at dinner parties, and why pronouns are equal parts helper and havoc-maker.

If grammar were a heist movie, the nouns would be the inside guys—steady, indispensable, pretending they're just along for the job—and the pronouns would be the getaway drivers. You'll want to keep an eye on both.

> In the 18th century, grammar books were considered "moral instruction"—because orderly sentences supposedly reflected an orderly mind.

Nouns Behaving Badly

What's in a Name?

At their core, nouns are deceptively simple. They're the names we give to everything that exists—and quite a few things that don't. People, places, ideas, emotions, dragons, existential dread—all nouns. They're the foundation of every sentence: the "who" or "what" we're talking about. Without them, verbs would have nothing to boss around.

But here's the twist: nouns aren't as stable as they look. They change roles, steal other words' jobs, and occasionally moonlight as adjectives. The word *chicken* can refer to a bird, a meal, or someone who won't enter the haunted house—all depending on context. Nouns are linguistic shapeshifters. They just wear name tags to make themselves look respectable.

In their best behavior, nouns keep things clear. In their worst, they turn prose into cluttered storage rooms of abstract jargon. When every sentence is loaded with *considerations, factors, issues,* and *concepts,* it's a sign that the nouns have unionized and kicked the verbs out. Strong writing needs nouns that *mean something*, not ones that hide behind inflated syllables.

So, what's in a name? Everything. But only if you choose it on purpose.

Instruction

A noun is any word that names a person, place, thing, idea, or feeling.

If you can put *the*, *a*, or *an* in front of it and it still makes sense, congratulations—you've probably found yourself a noun.

Examples:
- The dragon snored. ("The dragon" = noun)
- The fiery snore echoed. **Yes** ("Snore"—normally a verb—is acting as a noun.)

That's one of grammar's sneakiest tricks: words can swap teams. Sometimes a verb, adjective, or even a whole phrase moonlights as a noun—a phenomenon called **nominalization**.

Example:
- Verb: *We decided quickly.*
- Nominalized: *Our decision was quick.*

Same meaning, different energy. The first moves; the second poses for a group photo. You'll meet this trick again in the Verb chapter, but for now, remember that when actions turn into nouns, writing slows down. A little is fine—too much, and your prose starts sounding like a corporate memo written by ghosts.

The Takeaway

Choose concrete nouns whenever possible—things you can see, touch, or imagine—instead of abstract ones that vanish into the fog of *conceptual frameworks* and *implementation strategies*. If you're losing the thread of your own sentence halfway through, the nouns might be the culprits.

Try This

Take a paragraph of your own writing. Underline every noun. Now ask:
- Can I picture this thing?
- Is it concrete (*dog, candle, regret*) or abstract (*communication, awareness, enhancement*)?

If it's abstract, don't replace it—ground it. Add detail that makes it feel real or specific.

Example:

- Abstract: *Their communication improved.*
- Revised: *They finally stopped emailing in riddles and started talking like humans.*

Read it aloud. If it suddenly sounds like a real person said it—mission accomplished.

> The word *thing* once meant an assembly or council — like a Viking parliament. The *Icelandic Althing* (founded in 930 CE) literally means "The Everything."

Countable vs. Uncountable Chaos

You'd think counting would be simple. One apple, two apples. Easy. But then English, in its infinite mischief, throws in a few curveballs: one rice, two... *rices?* No. One information, two... *informations?* Definitely not. Suddenly, your grocery list sounds like performance art.

Welcome to the world of **countable and uncountable nouns**—a realm where logic goes to die and intuition tries to take over.

Countable nouns are the friendly, predictable sort. They play well with numbers and plural *-s* endings. You can have *one cat* or *three cats*, *a candle* or *a hundred candles* (especially if you're dramatic). They're concrete, tidy, and satisfyingly countable.

Uncountable nouns, on the other hand, are the free spirits of the language world. You can't stick a number in front of *water, furniture,* or *advice* without them giving you the side-eye. You can have *a glass of water* or *a piece of furniture,* but never *two waters* or *three furnitures*—unless you're in a diner or an IKEA warehouse, respectively.

This, by the way, is not because English wants to ruin your day. It's because some nouns represent things that exist as a *mass* or *concept*, not as individual units. Try separating "happiness" into chunks or "sand" into distinct pieces and you'll see the problem (and maybe question your life choices).

Instruction

A **countable noun** refers to something you can count as separate items: *book, pen, dragon, idea.*

An **uncountable noun** (also called a *mass noun*) refers to something you can't divide easily into individual units: *milk, furniture, air, music.*

Countable nouns can be used with *a/an* and can form plurals.

Uncountable nouns can't. They need **containers or measures** instead:

Examples:

- Countable: *A coin, two coins, three coins clinking in the jar.*
- Uncountable: *Some money, a bit of cash, a pile of treasure.*

Notice that *money* itself isn't countable—but the objects that represent it (*coins, dollars, rupees, doubloons*) are.

The problem is that some nouns like to **switch teams** depending on meaning:

Examples:

- *Chicken* (animal = countable): *Three chickens pecked at the fence.*

- *Chicken* (meat = uncountable): *We ate too much chicken.*
- *Hair* (collective = uncountable): *Her hair is shiny.*
- *Hair* (individual strands = countable): *There's a cat hair in my tea.*

So if you ever find yourself staring at a sentence wondering whether to add an *s*, ask yourself: am I talking about individual items or the general substance?

The Takeaway
When in doubt, **zoom in or out.**
If your noun refers to individual, separable things—count it.
If it's a mass, idea, or collective whole—measure it, don't count it.

And remember: adding an *s* doesn't make something plural if it was never plural to begin with. (*Knowledges* still isn't a word, no matter how many diplomas you have.)

Try This

1. Look at this list: *sugar, chair, hope, bread, cat, coffee, traffic, light.*
   Which ones are countable, uncountable, or both?
2. Rewrite these sentences correctly:
   - *She gave me an advice.*
   - *He bought three furnitures.*
   - *There was sand everywhere—tiny sands filled my shoes.*
3. Now try writing one sentence where a noun changes category depending on its meaning (like *coffee* or *experience*).

Collective Noun Conspiracies

If you've ever watched two English speakers from different sides of the Atlantic debate subject–verb agreement, you've already seen a collective noun conspiracy in action.

STEP AWAY FROM THAT SENTENCE

In North America, we usually treat groups as single units:
*The team **is** winning.*
*The band **sounds** great.*
Across the pond, though, they'll happily pluralize the whole lot:
*The team **are** fighting amongst themselves.*
*The band **have** just released a new album.*
Same words, different logic. Who's right?
Technically—both.
(And somewhere, an English teacher just fainted.)
Collective nouns—words that refer to groups of people or things acting as one—are slippery creatures. *Audience, family, committee, crew, staff, government...* all of them can swing singular or plural depending on whether you're emphasizing the group as a single unit or the individuals within it.

It's like the grammar version of a dysfunctional family: together in theory, divided in practice.

Instruction

A **collective noun** names a group of people, animals, or things considered as one unit.

Whether it's singular or plural depends on **how it behaves in your sentence.**

Examples:

- *The jury **delivers** its verdict.* (acting as one)
- *The jury **argue** among themselves.* (acting as individuals)

In American English, collective nouns are **usually singular.**
In British English, they're **often plural** when the members act individually.
Neither choice is wrong—just be consistent within your piece.
For fun, English also collects groups of animals under special "herd" names—technically countable nouns, but full of folklore:

- A *murder* of crows
- A *parliament* of owls
- A *crash* of rhinos
- A *flamboyance* of flamingos

Yes, those are real. And yes, someone was definitely having a day when they coined them.

The Takeaway

- Ask yourself whether your group is **acting together** or **acting separately.**
- Stick to one convention per manuscript.
- Don't overthink it—readers will notice meaning long before they notice grammar.

Quick trick: Replace the collective noun with a plural word. If it still sounds right, make the verb plural.

- *The committee **are** voting → The **members** are voting.* Yes

- *The committee **is** voting → The **members** is voting* **No** - *(sounds wrong → singular fits better)*

Either can work—it's about emphasis, not ego.

Try This

1. Pick one collective noun—*band, staff, team, crowd,* or *family.* Write two sentences using it as singular and plural.

*The staff **is** celebrating its success.*
*The staff **are** debating over who actually did the work.*

1. Now look at something you've written recently. Does it sound more natural to your ear in singular or plural

form?
Choose what fits the tone—unity or individuality.
2. Bonus challenge: invent your own "collective noun."
What would you call a group of editors? (*A panic? A red-pen riot?*)

So, we've survived the name game—from nouns that shapeshift, to ones you can't count, to entire collectives that can't agree on anything. You've met the words that name our world, define our chaos, and occasionally stage coups against verbs. The good news? You now know how to keep them in line. The next time you catch a sentence weighed down by abstract clutter or confused about whether a team *is* or *are*, you'll know exactly who's causing trouble—and how to fix it.

Now that we've named every dragon, emotion, and sandwich in sight, it's time to talk about the pronouns that replace them. Because once they start standing in for other words, things get personal.

Pronoun Panic

The Case of the Missing Antecedent

Pronouns are the understudies of language—always stepping in when a noun needs a break. They're the *he, she, it, they, who, which,* and *this* that keep your sentences from sounding like roll call at the National Association of **Redundancy** Association.

The wizard opened the wizard's spellbook because the wizard wanted to check the wizard's handwriting.

You get the idea. Pronouns save the story.

But for all their usefulness, pronouns are grammar's professional troublemakers. They move fast, change shape, and sometimes forget who they're standing in for. When that happens, we get the linguistic version of an identity crisis:

When Susan met her sister, she told her she was late.

Who's late? Susan? The sister? The pronoun refuses to say.

That's what we call a **vague or missing antecedent**—when a pronoun doesn't clearly point to one specific noun. It's the grammatical equivalent of shouting "Hey, you!" in a crowded room.

Instruction

A **pronoun** replaces a noun (the **antecedent**) to avoid repetition.

That shortcut only works if the reader can tell **exactly which noun** the pronoun stands in for. When two nouns could fit, the pronoun turns traitor.

Examples:

No - *Sok gave Harpur his map.* → unclear (whose map?)

Yes *Sok gave Harpur the map he had drawn.* → clear (the map belongs to Sok)

Yes - *Sok gave Harpur the map that belonged to Harpur.* → clear (the map belongs to Harpur)

Yes - *Sok handed Harpur a map of Harpur's lands.* → even clearer—no guesswork.

Another example:

No *When Anayah visited Yna, she was tired.* → unclear (who's tired?)

Yes - *When Anayah visited Yna, Anayah was tired.* → clear

Yes - *When Anayah visited Yna, Yna was tired.* → also clear—just a different meaning.

When two nouns share the same pronoun option (*his, her, their*), repetition beats confusion every time.

Readers will forgive a double name; they won't forgive a detour through grammatical guesswork.

The Takeaway

Pronouns are like helpful interns: they make your work easier until they start taking credit for things they didn't do. Keep them supervised.

If you ever have to stop and reread a line to figure out *who* or *what* a pronoun refers to, your reader will too.

Try This

1. Write a two-sentence scene using at least three people. Read it aloud—do your pronouns clearly point to the right person every time?
2. Fix this line:

When the editor spoke to the author, she realized she was wrong.
(Who realized what? Rewrite so no confusion remains.)

1. Grab a paragraph of your own writing. Circle every *it, this, that,* and *they.*
If any could refer to more than one thing, give them a refresher course in specificity.

Me vs. I—A Love Story Gone Wrong

If grammar had a soap opera, *Me* and *I* would be the jealous co-stars—constantly competing for the same line and blaming each other when it goes wrong.

For years, teachers have scared writers into believing that *I* is the more "correct" choice. So now, instead of saying *"Me and my friend went to the store,"* people overcorrect and say things like *"He gave the report to Jim and I."*

That's not confidence—that's grammatical guilt.

Here's the truth: neither *I* nor *me* is fancier, smarter, or better. They just play different roles in the sentence. *I* does the action. *Me* receives it. That's it. No moral superiority attached.

Think of them like a pair of scene partners:
I takes center stage when the verb follows.
Me takes the bow when the action lands on it.

Instruction

Use **I** when the pronoun is the **subject** of the sentence (the one doing the action).

Use **me** when it's the **object** (the one receiving the action).

Examples:

- **Yes** - *I wrote the book.* (I = subject)
- **Yes** - *He called me.* (me = object)
- **Yes** - *Harpur and I went flying.* (together, they're the subject)
- **Yes** - *The villagers saw Harpur and me.* (together, they're the object)

No *He called I.*—wrong role
No *Me wrote the book.*—Harpur would be ashamed
A quick trick: remove the other person and see what still sounds natural.

Examples:

- *Harpur and I went flying.* → *I went flying.* **Yes**
- *The villagers saw Harpur and me.* → *The villagers saw me.* **Yes**
- *He gave the report to Jim and I.* → *He gave it to I.* **No** - (so "me" is correct)

If it sounds wrong when you say it alone, it's wrong in the pair.
The Takeaway
I isn't always the "proper" choice—it's just the **subject** form.
If you wouldn't say it when flying solo, don't say it in company.
And remember: confidence in grammar isn't about sounding formal; it's about sounding right.

Example:

- Pretentious: *Between you and I, this sounds sophisticated.* **No**
- Confident: *Between you and me, this sounds natural.* **Yes**

When you pick the right one, the sentence just *clicks*.
Try This

1. Fix the following sentences:
    - *The teacher gave Mark and I detention.*
    - *Me and Harpur saved the day.*
    - *The dragon followed Sok and I home.*
    - *Between you and I, that spell was a disaster.*
2. Say them out loud with the "remove-the-other-person" trick.
3. Now, write one sentence each using *I* as the subject and *me* as the object.
   Make them ridiculous—the sillier they are, the more likely you'll remember them.

Reflexives—Myself Is Not a Fancy "Me"

Ah, *myself*. The pronoun people reach for when they want to sound formal, polite, or like someone who owns multiple fountain pens.

"If you have any questions, contact myself."

"The report was prepared by John and myself."

It sounds elegant, right? Wrong. It's just a grammatical cat wearing a monocle.

Reflexive pronouns—*myself, yourself, himself, herself, itself, ourselves, yourselves, themselves*—have a **very specific job**: they point back to the subject of the same clause. That's it. They don't exist to make your emails sound fancier.

They're the mirrors of the grammar world. If you can't see the same subject reflected, it's not reflexive—it's just confused.

Instruction

Use a **reflexive pronoun** when the **subject and object are the same person or thing.**

Examples:

- **Yes** - *I taught myself how to fly.* (subject = object = same person)
- **Yes** - *She blamed herself for the chaos.* (both refer to the same

"she")
- Yes - *The dragon warmed itself by the fire.*

Do **not** use reflexive pronouns when there's no mirror effect.
Examples:

- **No** - *The report was prepared by John and myself.*
  Yes - *The report was prepared by John and me.*
- **No** - *Please email myself if you have questions.*
  Yes - *Please email me if you have questions.*

Here's the quick check:
If you can't replace *myself* with *me* (or *yourself* with *you*) without breaking the meaning, you're misusing it.
Examples:

- **Yes** - *I hurt myself.* (Reflexive—the action comes back to "I.")
- **No** - *He gave the gift to myself.* (Incorrect—the action goes to "me," not back to "he."
- **Yes** - *He gave the gift to me.*)

The Takeaway
Myself isn't a power-up version of *me*. It's a boomerang—it only works if it returns to the thrower.
Use reflexives when the sentence loops back on itself.
Use plain pronouns the rest of the time, and your writing will sound confident instead of over-polished.
Try This

1. Fix these sentences:
    - *The professor and myself graded the papers.*
    - *The dragon looked at myself in the mirror.*
    - *Please send the parchment to Arthur or myself.*

2. Write two correct examples of your own using *myself* properly—one serious, one ridiculous.
3. Bonus challenge:
Write one intentionally awful sentence using *myself* incorrectly, just to see if it makes your inner editor twitch.

Gender-Bending Grammar—The Singular "They" and the Modern Mindset

Few topics can start a grammatical fistfight faster than the singular *they*. Half the room calls it progress; the other half insists it's heresy. But the truth is, *they* has been quietly doing this job for centuries—long before social media made people pick sides.

If you've ever said,

Someone left their coat on the chair, congratulations, you've already used the singular *they*. And the grammar police didn't even show up.

English used *they/them/their* as gender-neutral pronouns as early as the 1300s. Writers like Shakespeare, Chaucer, and Austen all used it without fanfare or moral panic. (*"Every one to rest themselves betake,"* wrote the Bard himself, blissfully unbothered.)

The fuss came later, when Victorian grammarians decided language should reflect tidy, masculine order—because apparently *he* was enough for everyone. Spoiler: it wasn't.

Language evolves because people do. The singular *they* simply steps in where *he/she* feels clunky or where gender isn't known, specified, or relevant. It's both ancient and newly essential.

Instruction

Use **they/them/their** as singular pronouns when:

1. The person's gender is **unknown or irrelevant.**

Someone forgot their umbrella.

1. The person's gender is **nonbinary** or **not exclusively male/female.**

Eli said they're publishing a new book next spring.

1. You want to **avoid repetitive "he or she" phrasing.**

If a writer wants to succeed, they must learn to revise.

Consistency is key: once you choose *they* as a singular pronoun for a person, use it throughout your text.

And remember—even though *they* refers to one person, the **verbs stay in their usual plural form.**

They are happy (not "They is").

They were writing all night (plural verb, singular person—totally fine).

Examples

Yes - *If anyone needs me, they can find me in the library.*

Yes - *Morgan said they'll send the manuscript tomorrow.*

Yes - *No one wants to admit they forgot their password again.*

No - *Someone left his or her coat.* (Technically correct, stylistically painful.)

You can also use *themself* in informal writing to match singular *they*. It's gaining acceptance and already listed in many major dictionaries.

The Takeaway

The singular *they* isn't a trend—it's a return to sanity.

It allows for inclusion, precision, and plain common sense.

Grammar's purpose is to serve meaning, and meaning changes as people do. Using *they* correctly isn't "bending" grammar—it's letting it breathe.

So, if anyone still complains that *they* can't be singular, tell them this:

Language doesn't ask permission. It evolves anyway.

STEP AWAY FROM THAT SENTENCE

Try This

1. Rewrite these sentences using singular *they* correctly:
   - *If a reader enjoys this chapter, he or she should thank the author.*
   - *When a teacher gives his students feedback, he helps them improve.*
   - *Someone left his hat on the dragon.*
2. Write a sentence using singular *they* for a nonbinary character.
3. Challenge: Find a sentence from your old writing that uses *he/she*. Rewrite it with *they*. Notice how naturally it reads? That's evolution doing its job.

Possessive Mayhem—Whose Grammar Is It, Anyway?

Ah, *its* and *it's*—the identical twins that everyone mixes up, even after years of therapy.

On paper, they look almost the same. In practice, they couldn't be more different.

One shows **ownership**. The other just **shows off**.

Let's get this out of the way once and for all:

- **its** = possessive pronoun (shows belonging)
- **it's** = contraction (stands for *it is* or *it has*)

That's it. That's the whole war.

So why do people keep losing? Because English, in one of its less charitable moods, decided that possessives usually take an apostrophe (*the dragon's hoard, the wizard's staff*), **except** for this one. Apparently *it* wanted to be special.

Instruction

Use **its** (no apostrophe) when something *belongs to it*.

Use **it's** (with an apostrophe) when it means *it is* or *it has*.
Examples:

- **Yes** - *The dragon guarded its treasure.* (possessive)
- **Yes** - *It's been a long night of hoarding gold.* (it has)
- **Yes** - *It's a beautiful morning for mayhem.* (it is)
- **No** - *The dragon guarded it's treasure.* (means "it is treasure"—nonsense)
- **No** - *Its been a long night.* (missing the apostrophe for the contraction)

A quick test: whenever you write *it's*, read it as *"it is"* or *"it has."* If it doesn't make sense, ditch the apostrophe.

The Takeaway

Think of *its* like *his* or *hers*. None of them use an apostrophe—because they're already possessive.
(*Writing his' sword would scandalize even a barbarian.*)
So:
its → possession
it's → expression
Get that straight, and you'll instantly sound 37% more competent on the internet.

Try This

1. Fix the apostrophes in these sentences:
    - *Its about time the dragon cleaned it's cave.*
    - *The phoenix fluffed it's feathers before it took flight.*
    - *It's tail was longer than it's shadow.*
2. Write one sentence using *its* correctly and one using *it's*.
3. Bonus challenge: work both into a single (coherent) sentence.

Example:
It's a well-known fact that the dragon never polishes its gold.

identity crises, and the eternal *its vs. it's* debate that keeps editors up at night. You've learned when to repeat a name, when to mirror an action, and when to let *they* do what it's been doing gracefully for seven hundred years. In short: you've survived the trickiest, tiniest words in the English language—and you've earned bragging rights.

But before we march off to verbs and action, there's one last bit of mischief to tackle—the sneaky hybrids that blur the line between nouns and verbs. Gerunds and infinitives: the multitaskers of grammar. They don't just *act*; they *are*. Let's wade into that swamp next.

Gerund Grievances

When Verbs Moonlight as Nouns

Verbs are action junkies... until they put on a fake mustache and call themselves nouns. That's a **gerund**: a verb with an **-ing** ending acting like a **thing**—the subject, object, or object of a preposition.

Running clears my head. (subject)
Arthur loves flying. (object)
Harpur is great at glowering. (object of a preposition)

Gerunds are useful, but when too many of them pile up, your prose starts to feel like a spin class taught by a bureaucrat: a lot of **-ing**, not much moving.

Instruction
A **gerund** = verb + -ing used **as a noun**.
A **present participle** = verb + -ing used **as an adjective** (or in progressive verbs).

Quick tests to spot a gerund

- If you can replace the -**ing** word with **something/that activity/it**, it's probably a gerund.

Swimming helps me think. → *It helps me think.* **Yes**

- If it functions as **subject/object/object of a preposition**, it's a gerund.

After writing, she naps. (after **what**? → a thing: writing) **Yes**

- If it **describes a noun**, it's a participle, not a gerund.

*the **glowing** sword* (adjective) → participle **No** (not a gerund)

Gerund vs. participle contrast

- **Gerund (noun):** *Skipping breakfast annoys me.*
- **Participle (modifier):** *Skipping breakfast, I regretted my life choices.*

Examples

- **Subject:** *Arguing drains the room of oxygen.*
- **Direct object:** *They considered merging the chapters.*
- **Object of preposition:** *Before leaving, check the map.*
- **Predicate noun:** *Her favorite hobby is collecting old maps.*

Not gerunds (participles instead):

- *The **boiling** kettle screamed.* (adjective)
- *We were **boiling** water.* (progressive verb)

The Takeaway

If the -**ing** word is **a thing you can name**, it's a gerund.
If it's **describing** or **helping a verb**, it's a participle.
Use gerunds deliberately; a swarm of them can make sentences mushy.

Try This

1. Label each -**ing** word as **G** (gerund) or **P** (participle):
    - *Climbing is harder without coffee.*

- *The **shimmering** portal tempted us.*
- *They talked about **moving** to Epoh.*
- *We were **waiting** for the courier.*

2. Rewrite one gerund-heavy sentence from your own work to use a **stronger finite verb** instead.

*Our focus is **improving** clarity.* → *We **improve** clarity.*

1. Write one sentence that pairs both correctly: a **gerund** and a **participle** in the same line.

When Grammar Demands Custody of the Verb

Here's a sentence that looks innocent enough:
I appreciated you singing.
But wait—what exactly did you appreciate?

- The person?
- The act of singing?
- The fact that they had the nerve to do it at all?

This is where grammar rolls up its sleeves and mutters, *"Context matters, kid."*

When a **gerund** (that *-ing* word acting as a noun) follows a pronoun or noun, you have two options:

- Make the preceding word **possessive** (*your singing*), or
- Leave it **objective** (*you singing*).

Both are technically allowed—but they mean *slightly different things.*

Instruction
Use the **possessive form** if you want to emphasize the **action itself** (the singing, the running, the questionable decision).

Use the **objective form** if you want to emphasize the **person doing it** (you, him, her, them).

Examples:

- **Yes** - *I appreciated **your** singing.* → You're focusing on the act.
- **Yes** - *I appreciated **you** singing.* → You're focusing on the person and their involvement.
- **Yes** - *We laughed at **his** dancing.* → The dancing itself was funny.
- **Yes** - *We laughed at **him** dancing.* → His attempt was funny. (Tone shift: now we're mocking.)

Either works, but the possessive form (*your singing*) feels more formal or written, while the objective (*you singing*) feels more conversational.

In polished writing, **clarity trumps correctness**—so choose whichever makes your intent unmistakable.

The Takeaway

Possessive + gerund sounds cleaner in formal contexts (*your singing, their arguing, my forgetting*), but modern usage has relaxed.

If it reads naturally and communicates what you mean, you're golden.

Just don't mix the two: *I appreciated you's singing* is where we draw the line.

Try This

1. Rewrite each pair, choosing between **possessive** and **objective**:
    - (your/you) singing saved the ceremony.
    - We were amazed by (her/she) painting the mural.
    - (their/them) laughing broke the silence.
2. Write one sentence where the choice changes the meaning.

I didn't like his interrupting. vs. *I didn't like him interrupting.* (First: you disliked the act. Second: you disliked the person's behavior.)

1. Bonus challenge: use one in dialogue and one in narration—notice the shift in tone?

Gerund Overload—The "-ing" Swamp

Gerunds are wonderful. They let verbs moonlight as nouns, turning action into substance. But like most good things—caffeine, adjectives, or dragons—too much can turn your prose into chaos. When every sentence starts swimming in **-ing** words, your writing begins to sound like a yoga class in a wind tunnel.

Running, shouting, and gasping, the hero, clutching his sword, began sprinting toward the burning, crumbling tower, screaming.

Sure, technically that's English. But it's also a grammatical marathon with no hydration breaks.

The problem isn't gerunds themselves—it's **overuse** and **clustering**. When too many appear close together, they smother your verbs and dull the rhythm of the sentence. Readers start to skim, and your prose starts to wheeze.

Instruction

A good rule of thumb:

- **One or two –ing words** in a sentence? Probably fine.
- **Three or more?** Check your oxygen levels.

When revising, watch for these patterns:

1. **Stacks of gerunds or participles:**

She was laughing, crying, shaking, and gasping. → pick the strongest.
Yes - *She was laughing and crying at once.*

1. **Unnecessary "being" verbs:**

It was being said that the dragon was being seen near the cliffs. → **Yes** - *People said the dragon was spotted near the cliffs.*

1. **Gerund pileups that slow the pace:**

He started running before realizing he was forgetting something.
→ **Yes** - *He ran, then realized he'd forgotten something.*
The fix is simple: **use finite verbs** where possible. They drive action instead of describing it from the sidelines.

The Takeaway
Gerunds are like glitter—a sprinkle adds sparkle; a handful makes a mess.

Use them purposefully, space them out, and vary your sentence openings.

If you notice more *-ing* endings than periods on a page, it's time for a rescue mission.

Try This

1. Find a paragraph of your own writing. Highlight every **-ing** word.
   - Are they all necessary?
   - Can you swap a few for strong verbs or concise clauses?
2. Rewrite this sentence to improve rhythm and readability:

Turning, blinking, panting, and stumbling, she kept running through the blinding morning.

1. Bonus challenge: Write one "over-the-top" –ing sentence *on purpose*—then revise it into something crisp and powerful. Notice how much more energy your verbs carry when they're

not buried alive in gerunds.

To Verb or Not to Verb—That *Is* the Question

Ah, the **infinitive**—English's way of letting verbs laze around while pretending they're hard at work. When you add *to* in front of a base verb (*to run, to eat, to procrastinate*), it stops being an action and becomes an *idea of an action*. In other words, it's a **verbal noun**—a noun in disguise.

To err is human.
To write is divine.
To overthink every sentence is the editor's curse.

Infinitives are like verbs on vacation: they still want credit for doing something, but really they're just lounging around describing possibilities.

Instruction

Use an **infinitive** (*to* + *base verb*) as a **noun** when it serves as:

- The **subject** of the sentence:

To dream takes courage.

- The **object** of a verb:

She loves to read.

- The **object** of a preposition (rare, but dramatic):

He had no choice but to flee.

Infinitives can also **compete with gerunds** for the same role:
She likes singing.
She likes to sing.
Both work, but the nuance shifts slightly.

- The **gerund** (*singing*) emphasizes the *activity itself.*

- The **infinitive** (*to sing*) emphasizes *the idea or intention of the act.*

He stopped smoking. → He quit.
He stopped to smoke. → He paused what he was doing to light up.
A single word changed, and so did his life expectancy.

The Takeaway

Infinitives and gerunds are like rival performers in the same show—both can take center stage, but their monologues are different.

When you want to express a habit or activity, reach for the **gerund.**

When you want to express purpose, preference, or potential, reach for the **infinitive.**

(*She enjoys writing,* but *she hopes to publish.*)

Try This

1. Complete the sentences with either a **gerund** or an **infinitive**, depending on the meaning:
    - She remembered _____ (feed) the dragon.
    - She remembered _____ (feed) the dragon last night.
    - I love _____ (write) at night.
    - I hope _____ (finish) this before dawn.
2. Rewrite one of your own sentences that uses a gerund—then try the infinitive version.
   Which one changes the tone or meaning more?
3. Bonus challenge: Write a sentence where both forms fit but mean different things—and make it funny.

> In the 14th century, English speakers briefly tried pluralizing *fish* as *fysshys*. The experiment failed, but it remains one of history's cuter linguistic uprisings.

The Bureaucracy of Words—When Verbs Get a Desk Job

If verbs are the doers of language, then **nominalizations** are the quitters—verbs that have traded their action for abstraction. They've stopped *doing* and started *existing* as concepts. It's like watching a once-vital adventurer retire into paperwork.

We made a decision. (nominalization of *decide*)
She gave a recommendation. (nominalization of *recommend*)
He performed an investigation. (nominalization of *investigate*)

Sure, they sound respectable. But too many nominalizations make your writing feel like it's trapped in a board meeting with no snacks.

An implementation of the policy was conducted following a consideration of circumstances.

Translation: *We thought about it and did it.*

Instruction

A **nominalization** happens when a **verb** (or sometimes an **adjective**) turns into a **noun**, often by adding endings like *-tion, -ment, -ance, -ity,* or *-ness*.

Common offenders include:

- *decide → decision*
- *analyze → analysis*
- *improve → improvement*

- *fail → failure*
- *happy → happiness*

Nominalizations aren't wrong, but they make writing feel passive and indirect.

The completion of the project was achieved by the team. → **No** - Bureaucratic sludge

The team completed the project. → **Yes**

Active, clear, human

Use nominalizations **sparingly**—they're fine in formal or abstract contexts (academic papers, legal documents, or when you want to sound Very Important™). Just don't let them smother your verbs.

The Takeaway

Nominalizations drain life from your prose faster than a vampire accountant.

If your sentence sounds like a memo or a mission statement, you've probably turned too many verbs into nouns.

Whenever possible, swap *"make a decision"* for *"decide," "perform an investigation"* for *"investigate,"* and watch your writing spring back to life.

Try This

1. Rewrite the following sentences to eliminate the nominalizations:
    - *The implementation of the plan was delayed by the consideration of options.*
    - *An observation of the stars was made by the student.*
    - *Her suggestion for improvement was appreciated.*
2. Pick one page of your writing. Circle every word ending in *-tion, -ment, -ance,* or *-ity.*
   Replace at least two with their original verbs.
3. Bonus challenge: Write one intentionally awful, nominalization-heavy sentence—then rewrite it to sound like

a human being again.

Example:
No - *The facilitation of the discussion was achieved through the allocation of time for communication.*
Yes – We talked it out.

You've made it through the grammatical gray zone—where verbs pretend to be nouns, nouns act like verbs, and sentences start to feel like identity crises in motion. From gerunds to infinitives to those abstract nominalizations that sound like they were written by a committee, you've learned to spot words that have given up the good fight of action in favor of just *existing*.

The good news? You now know how to bring them back to life. You can un-bureaucrat a sentence in seconds, decide when *to sing* or when *singing* sounds better, and keep your writing lean and lively.

So take a breath. You've mastered the naming words, the standing-in words, and the shape-shifting not-quite verbs.

Now it's time to get things moving.

Next up: the pulse of every sentence—the verbs. They'll leap, stumble, and sometimes refuse to behave, but one thing's certain... they'll keep the story alive.

Verbs—Movers, Shakers, and Rule-Breakers

If nouns are the bones of a sentence and pronouns the clever prosthetics, **verbs** are the muscle, blood, and caffeine. They make language *move*. Every story you've ever loved, every law you've ever skimmed, every text you've ever regretted sending—they all hinge on what someone *did, does, or will do*.

A world without verbs would be a world without motion.

The dragon... tower... smoke... despair.

See? Terrifyingly dull. Add verbs, and suddenly:

The dragon burst from the tower, scattering smoke and despair in equal measure.

Verbs are not polite creatures. They don't like sitting still, and they refuse to be predictable. They shift tense without warning, split infinitives like rebels, and occasionally stage mutinies against subjects that can't keep up. And that's exactly why we love them.

In this part, we'll wrangle:

- **Tense troublemakers** who twist time into knots.
- **Voice impostors** who swap active energy for passive padding.
- **Mood swings** that turn statements into questions, commands, or existential crises.
- And those rare, shining verbs that do nothing but *be*.

You'll learn when to let verbs lead, when to tie them down, and when to give them free rein. Because verbs don't just carry your sentence forward—they reveal its soul.

So grab your metaphorical lasso. It's time to tame the wildest part of speech in the English corral.

Tense Trouble—Time Travelers Anonymous

If verbs are the heartbeat of language, **tense** is its time machine. It decides *when* things happen—past, present, or future—and whether they stay there or get dragged kicking and screaming into another era.

Writers like to think they've mastered time. But tense has a way of turning even confident authors into confused travelers—jumping from *was* to *is* to *will be* faster than a toddler with a sugar high. One minute your dragon **burned** the village, and the next he **burns** it, and somehow by paragraph three he **will have burned** it already.

In short: tense is where clarity goes to die if you don't keep your verbs on a leash.

Instruction

A **tense** shows the **time** of an action or state of being.

There are three basic tenses—past, present, and future—and twelve standard combinations once you add aspects (simple, progressive, perfect, and perfect progressive).

The Core Three:

A tense shows the time of an action or state of being. There are three basic tenses—past, present, and future—and twelve total combinations once you add the aspects.

Past: *The dragon flew.* — Action completed.
Present: *The dragon flies.* — Action happening now.
Future: *The dragon will fly.* — Action yet to come.

But then grammar got fancy and added aspects—the part that tells how or for how long the action unfolds. That's when things start to feel like a grammar-themed episode of *Doctor Who*.

Each tense comes in four flavors—simple, progressive, perfect, and perfect progressive. Here's the quick cheat sheet before we dive deeper later on.

Aspect tells us how an action unfolds—its rhythm, duration, or persistence in time.

Simple: *She writes.* — Basic fact or habit.

Progressive (Continuous): *She is writing.* — Ongoing action.
Perfect: *She has written.* — Completed, but still relevant now.
Perfect Progressive: *She has been writing.* — Ongoing and still relevant.

Once you combine these with past, present, or future, you get twelve total possibilities—and roughly four hundred ways to confuse your readers if you aren't careful.

The Takeaway

You don't have to memorize the chart—you just have to control the *timeline*.

Stick with one tense per scene unless there's a deliberate reason to switch. Readers are surprisingly forgiving of dragons, time portals, and spontaneous combustion—but not of verbs that can't make up their minds.

Try This

1. Take a short paragraph from your writing.
    - Identify the main tense.
    - Highlight any verbs that break the timeline without reason.
    - Rewrite for consistency.
2. For fun, rewrite a single sentence in all twelve tenses:

The dragon eats the knight.

You'll either learn something profound or summon a linguistics professor. Possibly both.

Past, Present, and Future Walk Into a Bar

The past, present, and future walk into a bar.
The bartender looks up and says, "I'm tense already."

STEP AWAY FROM THAT SENTENCE 37

Welcome to the three pillars of time—the places every verb lives. Understanding these isn't just about labeling *when* something happens; it's about choosing *how the reader experiences it.*

Writers often think of tense as grammar's calendar system—yesterday, today, tomorrow—but it's also a mood setter, a tone shifter, and sometimes, a total plot saboteur. Let's break down how each tense pulls its own narrative tricks.

The Past Tense—Where Most Stories Live

Past tense is the storyteller's default mode. It feels natural because it mirrors how we think about life: something happened, and now we're talking about it.

It's dependable, clear, and keeps the reader grounded—unless you let it start time-traveling on its own.

Examples:

- *The dragon flew over the valley.*
- *Arthur raised his sword.*
- *Sok regretted nothing—except trusting Harpur to drive.*

Past tense gives readers the comfort of hindsight. But beware the **accidental tense shift**, where a sentence slides into present out of excitement:

No - *The dragon flew over the valley and breathes fire at the castle.*
Yes - *The dragon flew over the valley and breathed fire at the castle.*

Keep your verbs on the same timeline unless you're deliberately flashing forward.

The Present Tense—The Pulse of Now

Present tense puts readers right in the action. It's urgent, cinematic, and unfiltered—like they're standing beside the narrator as events unfold.

Examples:

- *The dragon circles overhead, her wings blotting out the sun.*

- *Arthur grips his sword tighter. He hopes this time she'll listen.*

It's great for immediacy but tricky to sustain. One wrong shift into past, and the illusion breaks. Too much of it, and readers may feel trapped in a never-ending moment.

Best used for:

- Personal essays or memoirs that want intimacy.
- Action scenes that thrive on immediacy.
- Stylized narration or experimental fiction.

The Future Tense—The Seer's Curse

The future tense is less common in storytelling because it predicts rather than describes. It's prophecy, promise, or threat.

Examples:

- *The dragon will burn the village by dawn.*
- *They will rebuild. They always do.*

Use it sparingly. Too much, and your prose starts sounding like an ominous weather report.

The future tense shines in dialogue, foreshadowing, or philosophical narration—moments where the speaker peers ahead rather than acting now.

The Takeaway

Each tense sets a stage:

- **Past** invites reflection.
- **Present** creates immediacy.
- **Future** builds anticipation.

Once you pick one, **commit**—at least for a scene. Time travel is cool in science fiction, but in grammar, it's usually a continuity error.

Try This

1. Write the same one-sentence story in all three tenses:

The knight kisses the dragon.
Notice how the tone shifts? One sounds nostalgic, one alive, one fated.

1. Take a paragraph of your writing and rewrite it in a different tense.
   Which version hits harder? Which one sounds forced?
2. Bonus challenge: Write a three-sentence micro-story—one in each tense—that still makes sense together. (It's trickier than it sounds!)

Perfectly Imperfect—The Trouble With Aspect

If tense tells us *when* something happens, **aspect** tells us *how* it happens.

Was it ongoing? Completed? Still echoing in the background like a bad decision?

Aspect is the nuance in time—the part of grammar that lets you say not just *when*, but *how long, how often*, or *whether the action's ghosts still haunt the present*.

Unfortunately, it's also the reason writers accidentally make their timelines sound like a soap opera recap.

The Four Aspects of Time

You already know the three basic tenses—past, present, and future. Each of those has four possible aspects, and together they form the twelve main verb forms in English. Think of them as different camera angles on time.

Simple: *I write.* — A fact, habit, or single event.
Progressive (Continuous): *I am writing.* — Ongoing action, in motion.

Perfect: *I have written.* — Completed, but still relevant now.
Perfect Progressive: *I have been writing.* — Ongoing and still relevant—mid-action with history.

Each one layers detail onto your timeline. Let's unpack them.

1. The Simple Aspect—Clean, Classic, Confident

The simple aspect gets straight to the point. It's uncluttered and doesn't apologize for being efficient.

The dragon sleeps.
The dragon slept.
The dragon will sleep.

Simple verbs state facts. They don't bother with context—just who did what, and when.

2. The Progressive Aspect—Caught in the Act

Progressive (or continuous) verbs show *incomplete* or *ongoing* action.

The dragon is sleeping. (right now)
The dragon was sleeping when we arrived.
The dragon will be sleeping during the eclipse.

They're great for painting motion and immediacy, but watch for **progressive overkill**—the *was being done* syndrome that drains momentum.

No - *He was being watched by the guards who were being distracted by the noise.*
Yes - *The guards watched him, but were distracted by the noise.*

3. The Perfect Aspect—The Ghost of Actions Past

Perfect tenses connect *two points in time*—something started earlier and still matters now.

She has written three novels. (finished them, but it's relevant now)
She had written three novels before she met her editor.
She will have written three novels by next year.

Each version ties the event to a reference point—past, present, or future—creating that sense of lingering impact.

When used right, perfect tenses add texture. When overused, they make writing sound like a tax form.

4. The Perfect Progressive Aspect—The Long Game

This one's the marathoner: a combination of continuity and completion.

He has been writing since dawn.
She had been flying for hours before landing.
They will have been studying for months by exam day.

It's useful when duration matters—when you want readers to *feel* the passage of time.

But use it sparingly. Too much, and your verbs start gasping for breath.

The Takeaway

Aspect is grammar's way of zooming in and out of time.

Use the **simple** when clarity matters, the **progressive** for action, the **perfect** for reflection, and the **perfect progressive** when you want to show endurance or ongoing chaos.

If you ever catch yourself writing *had been being*, that's the universe telling you to go outside.

Try This

1. Write one sentence in each of the four aspects using the same verb.

To breathe, for example:

- Simple: *She breathes fire.*
- Progressive: *She is breathing fire.*
- Perfect: *She has breathed fire before.*
- Perfect Progressive: *She has been breathing fire all morning.*

1. Rewrite a paragraph from your work that mixes aspects inconsistently. Simplify it.

2. Bonus: Write one sentence using every aspect correctly in order. It'll sound ridiculous—but you'll remember it forever.

When Time Slips—Avoiding Accidental Tense Shifts

Few things break a reader's immersion faster than an unplanned leap through time. One minute the hero **ran**, the next she **runs**, and before anyone can blink she **will have been running** since chapter three. Accidental tense shifts are like potholes in prose—tiny, jarring, and impossible to un-feel once you hit them.

Most tense slips aren't ignorance; they're *emotion*. You get caught up in the story's energy and your verbs follow your excitement instead of your outline. The problem is, readers don't experience your adrenaline—they just feel the whiplash.

Instruction

A **tense shift** occurs when a sentence or paragraph switches time frames **without warning or reason.** Intentional shifts are fine—flashbacks, reflections, prophecy—but accidental ones confuse the timeline.

Examples:

No - *The dragon **landed** on the tower and **breathes** fire through the window.*

Yes - *The dragon **landed** on the tower and **breathed** fire through the window.*

No - *Arthur **raises** his sword and **swung** at the beast.*

Yes - *Arthur **raises** his sword and **swings** at the beast.*

The key is consistency: if a scene starts in past tense, **stay there** until something deliberate changes it. If you want to switch, give readers a signal—a line break, a transitional phrase, or a clear shift in perspective.

How to Spot Time Travel You Didn't Mean

1. **Underline every verb** in a paragraph.
   If you see *was / is / will be* all cuddled up together, someone's

STEP AWAY FROM THAT SENTENCE 43

broken the space-time continuum.
2. **Read aloud.** The ear catches temporal jumps faster than the eye.
3. **Check dialogue tags.** Authors often fix dialogue in present tense and forget the tags are past:

No - *"I hate dragons," she **says**.*
Yes - *"I hate dragons," she **said**.*

1. **Beware copy-paste revisions.** Half-rewritten sentences can leave one verb stranded in another century.

Intentional Time Travel (The Right Kind)
Sometimes you *do* want to move between tenses—flashbacks, internal monologues, or predictive narration. Just flag it clearly:
*She remembered how it **felt** when Harpur **was** gone. Tomorrow, she **will face** him again.*
Clean transition. The reader stays oriented; the time jump lands smoothly.

The Takeaway
Consistency isn't boring—it's invisible. That's what makes it powerful.
If your verbs can hold a straight timeline, your reader can relax and follow the story instead of recalculating its chronology.
Save your time travel for the plot, not the prose.

Try This

1. Take one of your older paragraphs and mark the main tense. Fix any verbs that don't match.
2. Rewrite this disaster so it makes temporal sense:

He runs into the cave, found the treasure, and will celebrate later.

1. Bonus: Write a two-sentence flashback that uses a deliberate, graceful tense shift.
Make sure the reader knows exactly *when* they are.

Flashbacks and Foreshadowing—Playing With Time on Purpose

Once you've mastered keeping your timeline consistent, you earn your **time traveler's license.** Now you can break the rules—as long as you do it *on purpose.*

Flashbacks and foreshadowing are the narrative equivalent of time manipulation. Used well, they add emotional depth, mystery, and context. Used badly, they read like a bad edit.

The Flashback: Diving Into the Past

A **flashback** lets readers step backward in time to witness something that explains or deepens the current moment.

The trick? Make the shift *obvious*. Readers can handle a jump through time—they just need a map.

Cues that signal a flashback:

- Transitional phrases: *Years earlier..., Back when dragons still ruled the skies...*
- A change in verb tense: from **past** to **past perfect** (*had + past participle*)
- Sensory triggers: *She touched the amulet and remembered...*

Example:
The village burned around her. She clutched the amulet, remembering when her father **had given** *it to her under the same crimson sky.*

Once the flashback is done, return readers gently to the original timeline:

The memory faded. The fire was real now.

The Foreshadowing: Whispering to the Future

STEP AWAY FROM THAT SENTENCE 45

Foreshadowing plants subtle hints about what's to come.
It's not just about plot—it's about *tension management*.
Handled deftly, it creates a feeling of inevitability. Handled badly, it feels like the author is elbowing you in the ribs.

Example:
She didn't know it yet, but the next time she saw the amulet, it would glow red.
He told himself the bridge would hold. He should've known better.

Use **future tense** or **modal verbs** (*would, could, might*) sparingly to nod at the horizon without dragging the reader there prematurely.

Mixing the Timelines (Without Losing the Reader)

1. **Keep the main tense dominant.** Your story's "now" should anchor everything.
2. **Use perfect tenses for clarity.** They help mark what's already finished or what's still to come.

*She **had fought** the beast before.* → past before the past.
*She **will have won** by the time the moon rises.* → future before the future.

1. **Signal the shift, then commit.** Don't flicker back and forth. Stay in the flashback until it's complete, then guide readers home.
2. **Emotional continuity matters more than grammatical precision.** A smooth emotional flow forgives the occasional technical wobble.

The Takeaway

Flashbacks and foreshadowing are where grammar and storytelling shake hands.

They're proof that tense isn't just about correctness—it's about control.

When you command time, you control tension. When you control tension, you own the reader.

So break the rules—just make it look intentional.

Try This

1. Write a short scene in the past tense. Then add a single paragraph flashback using past perfect (*had + past participle*). Smoothly return to the main timeline.
2. Add one foreshadowing sentence to the same scene. Make it subtle enough that you could miss it on first read.
3. Bonus: Rewrite a flat scene from your book with one well-placed flashback or hint of future consequence. Notice how it deepens the moment without adding new plot.

Congratulations, Chronomancer of Grammar—you've survived the temporal turbulence. You now understand that tense isn't just about *when* something happens, but *how readers experience it*. You can travel between centuries, slip into memory, or glimpse the future—all without dropping your reader into grammatical vertigo.

The rules are simple:

- Pick your **timeline** and honor it.
- Shift only with purpose—never by accident.
- Let **aspect** fine-tune the pacing.
- And when in doubt, choose clarity over cleverness.

A story with clean, deliberate tense feels effortless, even when it's complex.

A story with sloppy tense feels like an author arguing with a time machine.

So claim your license. You've earned it. You can now bend time, flash back, flash forward, and loop your narrative around itself—as long as you make the reader feel safe in your hands.

STEP AWAY FROM THAT SENTENCE 47

Now that you've mastered movement through time, it's time to tackle movement through **voice**—the difference between doing the thing and having the thing done *to you*.

Next stop: **Voice Control—The Power and Peril of Active vs. Passive.**

Voice Control—The Power and Peril of Active vs. Passive

If tense is grammar's timeline, **voice** is its attitude.
> It decides whether your subject *takes action* or *takes a beating*.
> In **active voice**, the subject does the doing.
> *The dragon incinerated the village.*
> In **passive voice**, the action happens to the subject.
> *The village was incinerated by the dragon.*
> Same event, different energy. One feels cinematic; the other feels like a crime report.
> Neither is wrong—but one usually gets you published faster.

Instruction
> **Voice** is determined by whether the subject acts (**active**) or is acted upon (**passive**).

Voice	Example	Effect
Active	*Arthur swung his sword.*	Direct, dynamic, clear.
Passive	*The sword was swung by Arthur.*	Slower, formal, less immediate.

Active voice keeps your prose lively and transparent. Passive voice, when used strategically, can emphasize the receiver or conceal the doer (handy for mystery, bureaucracy, and apologies).

Why Writers Slip Into the Passive Without Noticing

1. **Fear of assigning blame.**

Mistakes were made. (by whom?)

1. **Desire for formality.**

The proposal was submitted. (sounds official, but lifeless)

1. **Academic conditioning.**

The experiment was conducted. (thanks, science)

1. **Habit.** Some verbs just *invite* it.

He was born. (fine)
He was celebrated by the crowd. (meh)

When Passive Voice Works

Despite its bad reputation, passive voice isn't evil—just easily abused. Use it when:

- The actor is unknown or irrelevant:

The jewels were stolen at dawn.

- The focus belongs on the receiver:

The treaty was signed by two nervous kings.

- You're going for formal or detached tone:

The sentence was commuted by royal decree.

Just don't let it take over. Too many "was" and "were" constructions make prose read like it's wearing concrete boots.

How to Spot (and Fix) Passive Voice

1. **Find "to be" verbs** (*is, was, were, been, being*) followed by a

STEP AWAY FROM THAT SENTENCE 49

past participle (*-ed* word).
2. **Ask:** "Who's doing the action?"
If the answer hides at the end of the sentence (after *by*), you're in passive territory.
3. **Flip it:**

No - *The spell was cast by the apprentice.*
Yes - *The apprentice cast the spell.*
The Takeaway
Active voice is confidence on the page. It's the writer saying, *I know who did what and I'm not afraid to say it.*

Passive voice, in small doses, has its place—but overuse makes writing sound like it's been wrapped in bubble wrap for safety.

Good writing isn't *always* active. It's *aware*.

You control the energy; don't let your verbs drift into witness-protection mode.

Try This

1. Rewrite the following into active voice:
   - *The ball was dropped by the player.*
   - *The prophecy was forgotten by the elders.*
   - *The cookies were eaten by someone not admitting it.*
2. Now rewrite one sentence in passive voice **on purpose**—to emphasize the receiver.
   - *The hero was betrayed by his own reflection.*
3. Bonus: Take a page of your writing and highlight every "was" or "were."
Turn half of them into actions. Watch your prose start breathing again.

The Accidental Villain—When Passive Voice Sneaks In

Writers rarely *choose* passive voice. It usually just... happens. Like losing your keys or agreeing to "just one more" round of editing.

It's the grammatical equivalent of fog: it softens edges, obscures responsibility, and makes your prose feel polite but powerless.

How It Sneaks In

1. **When the subject disappears mid-sentence**

The report was completed. (by whom?)
The writer knows who did it—the reader doesn't.

1. **When the sentence gets too long to manage**

The dragon was thought to have been seen near the mountain by some villagers who were concerned for their safety.
By the end of that, no one remembers who's doing the thinking, the seeing, or the panicking.

1. **When "to be" verbs take over**
   Is, was, were, been, being—they're useful, but like toddlers, they need supervision.
2. **When the writer is trying to sound formal**

The announcement was made. (Instead of *They announced it.*)
Bureaucrats love this trick. So do insecure authors.

Why It Matters

Passive voice creates **distance**—sometimes useful, often deadly.

When every sentence hides the doer, your reader starts to feel like no one's steering the ship.

The dragon was defeated by the hero. → Hero feels secondary.
The hero defeated the dragon. → Power restored.

STEP AWAY FROM THAT SENTENCE   51

Even subtle passivity can dull a scene's edge. Readers may not spot the grammar, but they'll *feel* the drag.

How to Kick It Out

- **Name the culprit.** Ask who's doing the action and put them first.
- **Shorten the sentence.** Long clauses breed passivity.
- **Replace "was" with something alive.**

The castle was cold. → *Frost crept along the stones.*

When Not to Panic

Sometimes passive voice is the right tool. It just shouldn't be the *default*.

The kingdom was saved.—Lovely, when we already know who saved it.

He was born.—Grammatically passive, stylistically fine.

Dinner was served.—Elegant, succinct, and perfectly appropriate (especially if you're writing Jane Austen fanfic).

The Takeaway

If you can swap your sentence around and make it livelier, do it.

If not, leave it be. The goal isn't to eliminate passive voice—it's to use it with intent.

Think of it as the minor key in your prose symphony: haunting, rare, and devastating when played at just the right moment.

Try This

1. Write one paragraph full of passive voice—then rewrite it entirely in active.
   Compare how the tone changes.
2. Find a line in your writing that's technically passive but emotionally right.
   Circle it. That's called *authorial instinct*.
3. Bonus: Read a page of your favorite book and highlight every

passive construction.

Even the greats use it—they just do it on purpose.

Balancing Act—When Passive Voice Deserves a Seat at the Table

Passive voice has taken a beating (ironically, in passive voice), so let's set the record straight: it's not the villain. It's just the **quiet guest** who only speaks when it has something important to say.

Used wisely, it can be powerful, elegant, and emotionally precise. The trick is knowing *when* to let it take the mic.

When Passive Voice Shines

1. When the actor doesn't matter

Sometimes the *action* or *outcome* is the point—not who did it.

The castle was destroyed before dawn.

The identity of the culprit might be irrelevant (or deliberately mysterious).

2. When you want emotional distance

Passive voice lets you cool a scene down, stepping back from pain or chaos.

Mistakes were made.

Her heart was broken.

It's understated, almost numb—perfect when your character can't bear to face the subject head-on.

3. When you want to sound formal or objective

Passive constructions are standard in journalism, science, and legal writing because they remove bias.

The samples were analyzed under controlled conditions.

The motion was denied by the court.

You can also use this tone in fiction when your narrator's professionalism or detachment is part of the voice—think of a historian, scientist, or weary god recounting events.

4. When the rhythm demands it

STEP AWAY FROM THAT SENTENCE

Sometimes, it just *sounds better.* English thrives on rhythm, and passive phrasing can create a smoother cadence or a more poetic pause.
The stars were swallowed by dawn.
Beautiful. Intentional. Exactly as it should be.
Why Balance Matters
If every sentence screams for attention, your reader stops listening. Passive voice provides contrast—the quiet moments between explosions.
It softens prose, giving readers a breath before the next punch of active energy.
Writing is like music: you need your crescendos, but you also need your rests.
Quick Test
Ask yourself three questions:

1. Does this sentence feel **intentional**?
2. Does the **focus** belong on the receiver or the doer?
3. Does it **flow** better this way?

If you answer "yes" to any of those, passive voice gets a seat at the table.
If not—kick it back to the kitchen.
The Takeaway
Active voice propels. Passive voice reflects.
One drives the story forward; the other lets it sink in.
Together, they create prose that moves with both power and grace.
Master the balance, and your sentences will not just act—they'll *resonate.*
Try This

1. Rewrite a passage from your own writing, or from a favourite book, using passive voice to slow the emotional pace. Does it feel more introspective?

2. Alternate between active and passive in a single paragraph to shape rhythm and emphasis.
   3. Bonus: Find one moment in your current work-in-progress where *passive* voice makes the line stronger, not weaker—and own that choice unapologetically.

If grammar were a symphony, **voice** would be the conductor—deciding which instruments lead, which fall silent, and how loud the story gets.

Now that you've wrangled the difference between *doing* and *being done to*, you officially have the power to control tone, energy, and emotional impact with a single choice of phrasing.

Active voice is your megaphone.

Passive voice is your echo chamber.

Each has a purpose; both are tools of intent.

When you choose active, you seize authority.

When you choose passive, you guide reflection.

When you know *why* you're choosing either, you're no longer writing by accident—you're writing by design.

So the next time you hear a grammar purist declare, "Never use passive voice," smile like someone who's already burned that rulebook for warmth. You know better. You're not avoiding passivity—you're commanding perspective.

Now take a bow, maestro. The orchestra is ready for your next movement.

Mood Swings—Commanding, Questioning, and Declaring with Style

Verbs don't just tell you what happens—they tell you how the speaker *feels* about it.

That's mood: grammar's built-in emotional register.

STEP AWAY FROM THAT SENTENCE　　　55

It's the difference between:
You're coming with me.
Come with me.
If only you would come with me.

Same idea, three entirely different vibes—assertive, commanding, wistful.

Mood rarely gets the spotlight, but it quietly shapes tone, authority, and character voice. When used deliberately, it's one of the most subtle tools in your writing arsenal. When ignored, it turns prose into emotional beige.

Instruction

Mood expresses the writer's or speaker's attitude toward the action. English has three main moods (and a couple of eccentric cousins):

Mood	Example	Function
Indicative	The dragon sleeps.	States facts or asks questions.
Imperative	Wake the dragon.	Gives commands or instructions.
Subjunctive	If I were a dragon…	Expresses hypotheticals, wishes, or demands.
(Bonus) **Interrogative**	Is the dragon asleep?	Asks directly—technically part of indicative.
(Bonus) **Conditional**	The dragon would wake if you poked her.	Shows dependence on another condition.

1. The Indicative—Everyday Reality

The indicative is your default mode. It's how we state facts and describe the world as it is (or as we believe it to be).

The sun rises. The editor sighs. The coffee cools.

It's steady, clear, and useful about 90 percent of the time. Just be careful not to let everything stay in indicative—too much certainty can make writing sound monotone, like a GPS narrating your plot.

2. The Imperative—The Commander's Mood

The imperative gives orders, instructions, or strong advice. It's the personal trainer of grammar.

Write that sentence again.

Don't touch that comma.

Release the dragon!

It often drops the subject ("you") because it's implied. Imperatives create immediacy and urgency, which is great for directions, recipes, or motivational rants.

Use too many, though, and your prose starts to sound like an overcaffeinated drill sergeant.

3. The Subjunctive—Grammar's Drama Queen

The subjunctive expresses things that aren't real—wishes, hypotheticals, or polite demands. It's the *what if* mood, and it's the reason editors drink.

If I were taller ... (not *was*)

I suggest he study harder. (not *studies*)

Long live the queen!

Modern English is quietly abandoning the subjunctive, but writers shouldn't. It adds elegance, melancholy, and that delicious old-world weight. It's how you tell readers you're serious *and* stylish.

4. The Conditional—Grammar's What-If Machine

Conditional statements depend on cause and effect: something would happen if something else did.

If Harpur hadn't stolen the map, the forest would still be standing.

If I were a better editor, I'd delete fewer emails out of spite.

Conditionals create tension—they're the bones of consequence and regret. Used well, they make your prose sound thoughtful and layered.

Emotional Grammar—How Mood Builds Tone and Character Voice

Now that you've met the grammatical moods, let's look at how they *feel*.

STEP AWAY FROM THAT SENTENCE 57

Mood isn't just a function of verbs—it's the invisible current that carries tone and emotion through every line.

Mood and Tone: The Secret Partnership

Tone is how you sound. Mood is how your sentences make others feel.

You can't separate them. They work together like lightning and thunder—the effect follows the strike.

Indicative: *She's coming back.* → Calm certainty.

Imperative: *Come back.* → Urgent, pleading, or commanding.

Subjunctive: *If only she would come back.* → Longing, regret.

Conditional: *She would come back if he asked.* → Bittersweet inevitability.

Each line conveys the same information—but a completely different emotional truth.

Character Voice and Mood

If you want distinct character voices, teach them different moods.

- **The confident leader:** Lives in imperatives.
  Move. Now.
- **The dreamer:** Lives in subjunctives and conditionals.
  If I were braver, I'd ask her to dance.
- **The pragmatist:** Lives in indicative statements.
  We have five minutes and two working legs. Let's go.

Most characters drift between moods, but their default grammar often reveals their worldview. Writers who understand that can control tone without ever touching description.

Mood Shifts for Emotional Impact

Changing mood mid-scene can heighten emotion without melodrama.

She says she's fine. (Indicative)
Be fine. (Imperative)

If only she were fine. (Subjunctive)

That shift—from fact to command to wish—carries an entire emotional arc in three beats. No adverbs required.

The Takeaway

Mood shapes emotion.

Tense shapes time.

Voice shapes power.

When you master all three, you stop writing sentences and start conducting meaning.

Indicative for facts.

Imperative for action.

Subjunctive for longing.

Conditional for consequence.

Mix them intentionally, and your story stops telling—it starts *feeling.*

Try This

1. Write a short paragraph in indicative mood. Then rewrite it in imperative and subjunctive. Notice how tone transforms without changing the content.
2. Write three one-line mottos:
    - One that commands.
    - One that wishes.
    - One that wonders "what if."
3. Find one sentence in your current manuscript that could be more powerful just by switching mood. Rewrite it and listen to the emotional shift.
4. (Advanced) Pick a neutral scene—like doing laundry—and rewrite it in a mood that doesn't fit: a tragic subjunctive, a dramatic imperative. Notice how mood alone alters meaning.

STEP AWAY FROM THAT SENTENCE

By now, you've learned that verbs aren't just little engines of action—they're emotional chameleons. They don't only tell you what happens; they whisper how it feels.

Mood is where language meets psychology. It's what makes a sentence sound like a command instead of a confession—or a plea instead of a statement. It's the quiet force that turns plain grammar into personality.

So whether your sentence declares, demands, or dreams, the question isn't "Is this correct?"

It's "Does this sound like what I meant?"

When you control mood, you don't just write clearly—you write intentionally.

You stop letting grammar boss you around and start making it work for you.

Because that's what this whole book is really about, isn't it?

Not just following the rules—but knowing them well enough to bend them until they sing.

Now take a breath, stretch your fingers, and prepare for what comes next: **Modifiers.**

We've covered what words *do*—now it's time to explore how they decorate, distort, and occasionally derail everything around them.

> The word *dude* started as a 19th-century insult for overdressed city slickers. "Dudish" meant "foppish." Grammar's glow-up isn't the only one.

Verbals Gone Wild—The Feuding Family of

Gerunds, Participles, and Infinitives

If verbs are the action heroes of grammar, **verbals** are their rebellious teenage cousins—still verbs at heart, but refusing to follow the rules.

They act like nouns, adjectives, or adverbs, depending on their mood. They don't always agree on who they are, and half the time, they show up late to sentences wearing someone else's function.

Welcome to the family reunion.

1. Gerunds—The Nouns in Verb's Clothing

Gerunds look like verbs (*ending in –ing*) but behave like nouns. They're the "career changers" of grammar:

Swimming is fun.
I love editing.
Writing keeps me sane.

You can spot them easily—they answer **what**?
What keeps you sane? → Writing.

Gerunds let you turn actions into things. They're great for concision and rhythm—until they start breeding like rabbits. Too many "-ings" make prose sound like a hamster wheel.

No - *Running, jumping, shouting, and giggling filled the afternoon.*
Yes - *The kids ran, jumped, and shouted all afternoon.*
Pro tip: one gerund = graceful; five gerunds = grammar soup.

2. Participles—The Adjectives with Trust Issues

Participles are verbs moonlighting as adjectives. They modify nouns, describing what the noun *is doing* (or *has done*).

They come in two flavors:

- **Present participles (-ing):** *The crying child*
- **Past participles (-ed, -en, etc.):** *The broken window, the stolen crown*

The dragon, exhausted and smoldering, collapsed on the castle roof.

STEP AWAY FROM THAT SENTENCE

Beautiful, right? But participles have a dark side—the **dangling participle.**

That's when they attach themselves to the wrong noun and chaos ensues.

No - *Running for the bus, the rain soaked my hair.*
(It sounds like the *rain* was running.)
Yes - *Running for the bus, I got soaked in the rain.*

If your modifier seems to describe the wrong character, fix it before your readers imagine weather with legs.

3. Infinitives—The Grammar Purists' Darling

An infinitive is the *to* + *base form* of a verb—*to write, to eat, to sleep, to edit at 2 a.m.*

Infinitives act like nouns, adjectives, or adverbs.

To write is to breathe. (noun)
She had a book to read. (adjective)
He paused to think. (adverb)

They're clean, elegant, and precise—which naturally leads us to one of grammar's most infamous debates...

4. The Split Infinitive Showdown—To Boldly Go or Not to Go Boldly

Traditionalists insist you should never split an infinitive—that is, put a word between *to* and the verb:

No - *To boldly go*
Yes - *To go boldly*

But modern English laughs in the face of that rule.

Why? Because sometimes splitting the infinitive **sounds better** or **makes meaning clearer.**

She decided to quietly leave. (sounds natural)
She decided quietly to leave. (sounds like she made a polite decision, not a quiet exit)

So yes—split away. Just do it for rhythm or precision, not rebellion. Grammarians have bigger dragons to fight.

5. Helping Verbs—The Sidekicks

Helping verbs (also called **auxiliary verbs**) support the main verb by showing tense, mood, or voice.

Think of them as the Robin to your Batman—the ones doing the emotional labor while the hero takes the credit.

is, am, are, was, were, have, has, had, will, would, can, could, may, might, must, shall, should, do, does, did

They're small but mighty. Without them, English would crumble into ambiguity:

She going. → Confusing.

*She **is** going.* → Clear.

Just beware of **helping verb pileups:**

No - *He has been being trained to be able to help.*

If your sentence sounds like an HR memo written by a time traveler, simplify.

6. Modal Verbs—The Commitment-Phobes

Modal verbs (like *can, could, may, might, must, shall, should, will, would*) express possibility, permission, or obligation.

They're the wafflers of grammar—never fully committing to anything.

I can write. (ability)

I may write. (permission)

I must write. (obligation)

I should write. (guilt)

I might write. (procrastination)

Each carries a subtle emotional flavor—and an excuse. They let you hedge, soften, or imply doubt.

Too many, though, and your prose starts to sound like it's apologizing.

No - *I might possibly be able to consider agreeing.*

Yes - *I'll think about it.*

The Takeaway

STEP AWAY FROM THAT SENTENCE

Verbals are grammar's shapeshifters—versatile, powerful, occasionally treacherous.

Handle them well and your writing sings. Let them run wild, and your reader will need a machete.

When in doubt, ask:

- Is it **doing** something or **being** something?
- Does it **clarify** or **clutter**?

Verbals aren't your enemies—they're your drama troupe. They just need a director.

Try This

1. Write one sentence using all three types of verbals.

Running from the storm, she hoped to find shelter before drowning became her hobby.

1. Spot and fix the dangling participle:

Flying through the night sky, the castle looked tiny below the dragon.

1. Write three modal sentences that show growing reluctance:

I will go. I should go. I might go.

Verbals are grammar's shapeshifters—half verb, half something else entirely. They can turn action into identity, motion into description, and clarity into chaos if left unsupervised.

Treat them like magic spells: powerful in the right hands, disastrous in the wrong. Use them with precision, keep them grounded in purpose, and they'll make your prose hum instead of hiccup.

> The Oxford English Dictionary lists 645 distinct meanings for the verb form of the word run!

Irregular Verbs Anonymous—Patterns, Holdouts, and Pitfalls

Welcome to **Irregular Verbs Anonymous**, where English verbs gather in a dimly lit church basement to confess their crimes against logic.

"Hi, I'm *go*, and my past tense is *went*."

"Hi, *go*."

"I don't even know where *went* came from."

If you've ever wondered why we say *ran* instead of *runned* or *brought* instead of *brang*, you're not alone—even linguists mutter into their tea about this one.

The Problem with Irregular Verbs

Irregular verbs are the rebels that refused to evolve with the rest of the language.

Most verbs neatly add *–ed* for the past tense:

walk → walked

love → loved

But irregular verbs? They're the ones that kept their prehistoric roots, warping through centuries of sound changes like linguistic shapeshifters.

go → went

eat → ate → eaten

sing → sang → sung

STEP AWAY FROM THAT SENTENCE 65

They don't follow the rules—they *are* the rules' exceptions.

1. The Good News: There's a Pattern (Kind Of)
While irregular verbs look chaotic, many of them actually fall into loose families—phonetic patterns passed down from Old English.

Type	Example	Pattern
Vowel Change (Strong Verbs)	*sing → sang → sung*	The vowel shifts, consonants stay.
Same Form Throughout	*cut → cut → cut*	Efficient. Lazy. We respect that.
-t Ending Family	*keep → kept, sleep → slept*	Adds a soft –t instead of –ed.
Oddballs	*go → went, be → was/were → been*	No pattern. Pure anarchy.

If you can learn the patterns, you'll start spotting the logic hiding in the madness.

2. The Holdouts: Irregulars That Refuse to Die
Many irregular verbs have regular "wannabe" forms—ones people occasionally (and hilariously) invent.

No - *brang* instead of *brought*
No - *flied* instead of *flew*
No - *runned* instead of *ran*

The truth? English *used to* have hundreds of irregulars. Over centuries, most regularized themselves—but a few stubborn elites clung to their oddities, refusing to conform. They're linguistic aristocracy: nonsensical, powerful, and probably here to stay.

3. The Sneaky Semi-Regulars
Then there are the fence-sitters—verbs that are *partly* irregular or have multiple accepted forms:

dreamed / dreamt
learned / learnt
burned / burnt

Both are correct; one just sounds fancier depending on which side of the Atlantic you're on.

In general:

- **-ed** is North American.
- **-t** is British.

Choose one style and stay consistent unless your narrator's accent demands otherwise.

4. The Ultimate Wildcard: "To Be"

The verb **to be** is the most irregular word in English—and possibly the most ancient.

I am, you are, he is, we are, they are; I was, you were, he was; been, being...

It's a Frankenstein's monster stitched together from several ancient verbs meaning *to exist, to become,* and *to remain.*

It's so essential that English lets it break every rule, and we just nod along because, honestly, we need it too much to argue.

5. Common Pitfalls

Even strong writers trip over these classic irregular slip-ups:

Wrong	Right
I have drank too much coffee.	*I have drunk too much coffee.*
He had ran to the store.	*He had run to the store.*
They have went home.	*They have gone home.*
He has brang his notes.	*He has brought his notes.*

If in doubt, try reading it aloud. If your inner English teacher screams, trust her.

The Takeaway

Irregular verbs are living fossils—proof that language isn't a system; it's an ecosystem.

They remind us that grammar didn't come from a manual—it came from *people*, and people are messy.

STEP AWAY FROM THAT SENTENCE

So don't memorize every form; **get familiar** with the ones you use often.

The rest? Context and intuition will save you. And you can always refer back to this book!

When in doubt, consult a list, laugh at the absurdity, and move on. (And remember: it's *drunk*, not *dranked*. Unless you're in a bar joke, in which case all bets are off.)

Try This

1. Write a "meeting of Irregular Verbs Anonymous." Have at least three verbs confess their crimes.
2. Make a mini chart of five irregulars you use often—and their past and past participle forms.
3. Bonus: Try to invent a "regular" version of an irregular verb. (*Yesterday, I thinked hard.*) Then use it in a sentence. See? It sounds wrong because it *is*.

You've made it through the battlefield of verbs—tense, voice, mood, irregulars, and everything in between. If this were a video game, you'd be unlocking the Verb Whisperer achievement right about now.

Verbs are the pulse of every sentence—the spark where motion begins and meaning finds muscle. They can show strength, hesitation, regret, confidence, or confusion, often without you realizing how much they're doing. But mastery isn't about using more verbs; it's about using them on purpose.

Sometimes, the story calls for precision and power—a verb that stretches time, deepens tone, or tilts the rhythm just right.

Had been writing.
Might have been waiting.
To boldly go.
Was being followed.

These are not flourishes; they're focus pulls. You're shaping time, emotion, and heartbeat, one verb at a time.

Other moments call for simplicity. When you catch yourself writing *had been being trained to possibly start helping someday*, it's time for a linguistic exorcism. Simple verbs hit harder.

He went.

She ran.

They lived.

Simplicity isn't weakness—it's confidence. You trust your story to carry the weight without scaffolding.

The real art lies in balance. Strong writers shift gears—past to present, active to passive, declarative to hypothetical—always with intention. That's your job now: to flex when it matters, and to know when restraint speaks louder.

Because writing isn't about sounding smart. It's about sounding *alive.*

Verbs are your story's bloodstream. Keep them flowing, keep them honest, and above all, keep them *yours.*

When you write with clear verbs, readers trust you. When you write with deliberate verbs, readers feel you. And when you write with joyful verbs—the ones that leap off the page—readers follow you anywhere.

You've officially mastered motion.

Now stretch your fingers and prepare for what comes next: Modifiers. Because the only thing more dangerous than a rogue verb… is a dangling one.

Modifiers—Adverbs and Adjectives

If nouns are the bones of a sentence and verbs are the muscle, modifiers are the glitter—the shimmer, the polish, and, occasionally, the stray spark that blows the whole thing up.

But with great descriptive power comes great potential for disaster. For every writer who uses modifiers like careful brushstrokes, there's another using them like a glitter cannon. Too few, and your prose feels skeletal. Too many, and it suffocates under perfume and lace.

Modifiers are useful tools. The trick is learning when to let them sing and when to tell them to sit quietly in the corner. Used with intention, they shape tone and texture; used carelessly, they blur the very image they're meant to sharpen.

In this chapter, we'll explore the twin forces of modification: adjectives, which describe identity, and adverbs, which describe behavior. You'll learn how they work, how they work *together*, and how to keep them from staging a coup against clarity. By the end, you'll know not only how to wield modifiers—but how to make them earn their keep.

Because every writer loves a little glitter. Only the wise ones know when to stop shaking the jar.

The Modifier Showdown—Adjectives vs. Adverbs

Modifiers are the wardrobe department of language—their job is to dress nouns and verbs for the occasion. Adjectives add polish and personality, while adverbs throw glitter on the verbs (sometimes too much). But together, they can make even the plainest sentence sparkle—or look like it's late for a costume party.

Before we dive into the chaos, let's start with the first question every writer faces: how do you know when to use an adjective and when to use an adverb?

Let's break it down.

Modifier	Modifies	Example	Notes
Adjective	Nouns or pronouns	*A suspicious dragon glared at me.*	Describes a thing or being.
Adverb	Verbs, adjectives, or other adverbs	*The dragon glared suspiciously.*	Describes how, when, or to what extent.

It's a simple distinction—until English gets bored.

> "Awful" once meant "full of awe" — as in "awesome." When you say something's *awful*, you're technically expressing reverence.

How vs. What Kind—Choosing Between Adjective and Adverb

Instruction

Adjectives describe **what kind** of thing you're talking about.

Adverbs describe **how** something happens.

The difference sounds simple until your sentence starts playing dress-up with both at once.

Use adjectives to modify **nouns** (people, places, things).

Use adverbs to modify **verbs**, **adjectives**, or **other adverbs**.

Think of it this way:

- Adjectives talk about *qualities*.

STEP AWAY FROM THAT SENTENCE 71

- Adverbs talk about *manner*.

Examples
Yes - *She wore a beautiful dress.* → "Beautiful" describes the noun "dress."
Yes - *She sang beautifully.* → "Beautifully" describes the verb "sang."
No - *She sang beautiful.* → Grammatically incorrect—"beautiful" can't modify a verb.
Yes - *He's a quick runner.* → "Quick" modifies the noun "runner."
Yes - *He runs quickly.* → "Quickly" modifies the verb "runs."
Quick tip: if the word answers *what kind*, it's an adjective.
If it answers *how, when, where*, or *to what extent*, it's an adverb.

The Takeaway
Adjectives belong to things.
Adverbs belong to actions.
If you can't decide which you need, look at the word it's dressing—nouns wear adjectives; verbs wear adverbs. Mixing them up won't end the world, but it might make your editor twitch.

Try This
Underline every modifier in this sentence:
The dragon breathed fiercely as its purple wings beat against the smoky air.
Now label each as adjective or adverb.
Then rewrite the sentence using a different combination—make it sound calmer, or wilder, or absurdly poetic.
Ask yourself: did your modifiers help, or just add extra sequins?

When They Work Together

Instruction
Adjectives and adverbs don't always compete—sometimes they form alliances worthy of myth.

When used thoughtfully, the two can build layered, nuanced description without stepping on each other's grammatical toes. The trick is balance: one defines *what* something is, the other defines *how* it exists or behaves.

You can think of it as choreography:

- The **adjective** sets the scene.
- The **adverb** tells us how the scene moves.

Used together, they can turn a plain statement into a vivid moment.

Examples
Yes - *The bright sun shone warmly over the hills.*
→ "Bright" describes *what kind* of sun (adjective), "warmly" tells *how* it shone (adverb).
Yes - *She gave a quick, nervously polite smile.*
→ "Quick" and "polite" describe the smile (adjectives), "nervously" adds emotional context (adverb).
Yes - *He spoke in a low, soothing voice that carried surprisingly far.*
→ "Low" and "soothing" describe *voice*; "surprisingly" modifies *far*.
No - *The loudly singer sang beautiful.*
→ The adverb and adjective are misplaced; they should modify the *right* targets.
Yes - *The loud singer sang beautifully.*
→ Balance restored. Everyone can relax.

The key is precision. Each modifier must clearly attach to its intended word. Otherwise, your prose turns into grammatical spaghetti.

The Takeaway
Modifiers work best when they respect boundaries.
Adjectives paint the still image; adverbs direct the motion.

Together, they can enrich a scene—but if both fight for attention, the reader won't know where to look.

Use them like a duet, not a duel.

Try This

Take this sentence:

The knight looked brave and spoke confidently.

Now experiment:

1. Swap the order of the modifiers.
2. Add a second adjective or adverb to each clause.
3. Remove one modifier entirely.

Which version feels strongest? Which one feels overwritten?

Sometimes the most powerful partnership between adjectives and adverbs is the one where one steps quietly aside.

The Double Modifier Trap

Instruction

Stacking adjectives or adverbs might feel like adding flavor, but too many cooks spoil the syntax.

The double modifier trap happens when writers use two modifiers that repeat or contradict each other. It's the literary version of saying "free gift" or "completely finished." One word was enough; the second just shows up late to the party holding the same casserole.

The goal isn't to strip sentences bare—it's to keep them clean and deliberate. Every modifier should earn its place.

Examples

No - *She smiled happily.* → The smile itself implies happiness.

Yes - *She smiled.* → The adverb isn't needed; the verb carries the emotion.

No - *The small little house looked cozy.* → "Small" and "little" are synonyms—one can go.

Yes - *The little house looked cozy.*
No - *He whispered quietly.* → How else does one whisper?
Yes - *He whispered.*
No - *She absolutely insisted.* → "Insisted" already carries totality.
Yes - *She insisted.*
Yes - *He spoke softly but clearly.* → Different ideas, both useful.

The trick is to check whether your modifiers **add information** or merely **echo** it. If they're twins, let one go. If they're teammates, let them stay.

The Takeaway

Repetition doesn't intensify meaning—it dilutes it.

When modifiers double up, one usually exists to make the writer feel safer, not to make the sentence stronger.

If two words are saying the same thing, one of them is lying about being necessary.

Try This

Look at your current manuscript. Search for –ly words and adjacent adjectives.

Ask:

- Do they describe different ideas (tone vs. texture, emotion vs. motion)?
- Or are they clones in disguise?

Revise three sentences to remove redundant modifiers, then read them aloud.

If the rhythm feels cleaner and the meaning sharper, congratulations—you've escaped the trap.

The Stealth Adverb

Instruction

STEP AWAY FROM THAT SENTENCE 75

Adverbs are sneaky little shapeshifters. They don't always end in –ly, and that's where most writers get ambushed. Some slip quietly into sentences disguised as adjectives, prepositional phrases, or even nouns doing overtime.

The result? Confusion—and the occasional editor muttering into their coffee.

The key is recognizing when a word is *acting* like an adverb, even if it doesn't *look* like one. Remember: if it's modifying a **verb, adjective,** or **another adverb,** it's wearing the adverb badge, no matter what outfit it's in.

Examples

Yes - *He ran fast.* → "Fast" looks like an adjective, but it tells **how** he ran.

Yes - *She arrived early.* → "Early" answers **when,** not **what kind.**

Yes - *They worked hard all night.* → "Hard" modifies *worked*, not a noun.

Yes - *The dragon flew high above the clouds.* → "High" is an **adverb** describing **where** the dragon flew (its altitude).

No - *She sings beautiful.* → Wrong disguise—"beautifully" is needed here because it's describing *how* she sings, not *what kind* of singer she is.

And then there are the truly dangerous doubles—words that look identical whether they're adjectives or adverbs. Context decides their allegiance.

Yes - *He ran fast.* → "Fast" modifies the verb *ran* → adverb.

Yes - *He drives a fast car.* → "Fast" modifies the noun *car* → adjective.

Yes - *She arrived early.* → "Early" modifies *arrived* → adverb.

Yes - *Her early arrival surprised everyone.* → "Early" modifies *arrival* → adjective.

Same spelling, different jobs. Swap their roles, and the meaning doesn't just shift—it mutates.

The Takeaway

Not every adverb waves a shiny –ly flag. Some are undercover.

If a word explains *how, when, where,* or *to what extent* something happens, it's an adverb—no matter what its spelling suggests.

When in doubt, ask: "What is this word modifying?" If the answer isn't a noun, you've probably caught an adverb in the act.

Try This
Underline the adverbs in this sentence:
The wizard spoke softly, then vanished suddenly into thin air.

Now write your own sentence using at least one *stealth adverb* (like fast, late, near, or long).

Read it aloud—does the rhythm change if you swap it for an –ly version? Which one sounds truer to your style?

Bonus challenge: Find one of your old sentences with an adverb that's gone rogue. Catch it, name it, and decide whether it belongs or needs to be escorted off the page.

By now, adjectives and adverbs should feel less like rivals and more like co-conspirators. Each has its own job, its own territory, and its own bad habits. Used with care, they can illuminate meaning and rhythm; used recklessly, they can turn prose into a carnival parade. The trick is knowing who's dressing what—and when to tell them both to go change.

Adjective Addiction—When Description Turns Desperate

Adjectives are like frosting: a little makes the cake irresistible, but too much and everyone's just scraping it off. Writers love adjectives because they feel safe—like throwing a blanket of color and texture over a plain sentence. But the truth is, adjectives are sugar. They add flavor, not substance, and too many will rot your prose from the inside out. This section is your literary detox: a reminder that sometimes the strongest sentence is the one that trusts its nouns to speak for themselves.

The Adjective Pile-Up

Instruction

Adjectives are seductive little words. They whisper that one more will make your sentence stronger, brighter, more vivid. So you give in—*the long, winding, dusty, sun-baked road.* That's a map! It may paint a clear picture, but your reader will enjoy the journey more if it isn't condensed into a pile they have to trudge through all at once.

The problem isn't adjectives themselves; it's when they travel in packs. A single, well-chosen word can paint an image. A cluster of them muddies the view. Readers don't want to wade through description—they want to *see* it unfold.

If your sentence looks like a police sketch artist trying too hard, you've got an adjective pile-up.

Examples

No - *The tall, dark, mysterious, handsome stranger entered the smoky, dimly lit, crowded saloon.*

Yes - *A dark stranger stepped into the crowded saloon.*

No - *She carried a small, delicate, fragile, ancient teacup.*

Yes - *She carried an ancient teacup.* (If it's ancient, we can guess it's fragile.)

No - *The big, red, old, rusty truck rumbled down the road.*

Yes - *The rusty truck rumbled down the road.*

Adjectives work best when they reveal *something specific that matters*. If the word isn't doing emotional or sensory work, it's probably just hanging around for attention.

The Takeaway

Every adjective must earn its keep.

If it doesn't change the image, deepen the tone, or shift the meaning, it's filler—delete it.

Description should sharpen the reader's focus, not bury it under decorative debris.

The fewer adjectives you use, the more power each one has.

Try This
Pick a paragraph from your manuscript and highlight every adjective.

Now, for each one, ask:

- Does this add *new* information or just repeat what's implied?
- Could the noun or verb carry the meaning alone?

Cut half of them.

Then read the passage aloud—does it sound cleaner, bolder, more confident? Congratulations. You're in recovery.

Strong sentences build strong scenes. If you can declutter one line, you can declutter a paragraph—and your reader will thank you for the breathing room.

The Cliché Trap

Instruction

Adjectives love to hide inside clichés. They're sneaky like that—slipping into phrases that sound familiar enough to feel right but say absolutely nothing. When you describe a *cold, hard truth* or a *sparkling blue sky*, you're not painting a picture; you're hitting play on a recording everyone's already heard.

Clichés are the comfort food of writing—warm, predictable, and rarely nourishing. They sneak in when you reach for easy imagery instead of honest description. The goal isn't to make readers nod in recognition; it's to make them *see* what you see.

If your adjectives feel like they came from a motivational poster, it's time to send them packing.

Examples

No - *She gazed into his deep, blue eyes.* → How deep can eyes be? And what shade of blue are we looking at?

Yes - *His eyes were the blue of old denim—worn, soft, and familiar.*

STEP AWAY FROM THAT SENTENCE

No - *The bitter, cold wind bit her cheeks.* → "Bitter" and "cold" have lost their bite.

Yes - *The wind clawed at her face, tasting of iron and snow.*

No - *A tall, dark stranger entered the room.* → That stranger has been entering rooms since the 1800s.

Yes - *A shadow crossed the doorway—a man, taller than most, entered the parlor with assuming presence.*

Cliché adjectives feel safe because they've been tested a thousand times. But safety is the enemy of vivid writing. Replace the default image with one that only *you* could have written.

The Takeaway

Clichés aren't wrong—they're just tired. Your job as a writer isn't to repeat what's been said; it's to reimagine what's been seen.

If your adjectives could double as perfume names or weather reports, they probably need to retire.

Try This

Find a sentence in your work that includes a cliché adjective or phrase (*crystal clear, pitch black, red-hot anger,* etc.).

Now, dig deeper:

- What does that phrase *really* mean in your scene?
- What image or sensation do you want the reader to feel?

Rewrite it with fresh language that belongs only to your world.

Then read the two versions side by side. One will sound familiar. The other will sound alive.

The Order of Adjectives (Why "Green Little Men" Sounds Weird)

Instruction

English speakers follow an unspoken rule when stacking adjectives. We don't consciously think about it, but we *feel* it. That's why *"green little men"* sounds off, while *"little green men"* rolls right off the tongue.

Native speakers instinctively know the order—non-native speakers have the right to curse us for it. The rule goes something like this:

1. **Quantity or number** (three, several, many)
2. **Opinion or quality** (lovely, horrible, shiny)
3. **Size** (tiny, enormous)
4. **Age** (old, young, ancient)
5. **Shape** (round, square, flat)
6. **Color** (red, green, blue)
7. **Origin** (French, Martian, Canadian)
8. **Material** (wooden, silk, metal)
9. **Purpose** (sleeping bag, writing desk, racing car)

Yes, it's ridiculous. No, there's no good reason for it. It's just how English evolved, and it's one of the many reasons grammar teachers drink.

Examples

Yes - *A lovely small old round green French wooden writing desk* → Technically correct (though no one should ever write this sentence).

No - *A French green wooden old small writing lovely desk* → Grammatically "right," emotionally catastrophic.

Yes - *She adopted a tiny black rescue cat.* → *Size → color → purpose.*

No - *She adopted a rescue black tiny cat.* → It sounds like you're describing a disobedient cat who defied rescue efforts.

Yes - *The ancient silver dragon slumbered on his treasure.* → *Age → color → noun.*

No - *The silver ancient dragon slumbered on his treasure.* → Something just feels... wrong.

STEP AWAY FROM THAT SENTENCE

The rule is ancient instinct now. It's rhythm. It's musicality. Break it only when you *want* the reader to stumble—and even then, know exactly why you're doing it.

The Takeaway

Word order is the quiet architecture of English. You don't notice it until someone builds the walls in the wrong order.

You can paint your sentences however you like, but ignore the blueprint at your peril.

If it sounds weird, it probably *is*.

Try This

Write a sentence with **three adjectives** before a noun.

Now scramble the order and read both versions aloud.

Which one sounds natural? Which one makes you tilt your head like a confused dog?

That's the rule in action—proof that grammar sometimes operates on gut instinct and fairy dust.

When to Keep Them

Instruction

After all this talk of trimming, you might be afraid to use adjectives at all—as if the grammar police will break down your door and confiscate your thesaurus. Relax. Adjectives aren't villains; they're just powerful tools that need adult supervision.

A good adjective earns its spot by revealing something the noun or verb alone can't. It deepens meaning, sharpens tone, or gives the reader emotional context. The trick is to know when the modifier *serves* the sentence rather than *showing off* in it.

The best adjectives do one of three things:

1. **Change the image.** (*A crimson sky* paints something new, not just *a red one*.)
2. **Add mood or emotion.** (*A lonely road* feels different from *a*

long road.)
3. **Shift interpretation.** (*An imaginary friend* isn't just a friend—it's a clue to the story.)

If it doesn't do any of those, it's probably loitering.

Examples
Yes - *He opened the empty box.* → "Empty" adds meaning—without it, we don't get the disappointment.
Yes - *She wore her mother's faded wedding dress.* → "Faded" turns nostalgia into loss.
Yes - *They huddled beneath the broken sign.* → "Broken" changes the entire atmosphere.
No - *The big, tall man walked slowly across the wide, open field.* → Not one of those adjectives makes us care more.

Good adjectives are emotional cues, not decorative confetti. They help the reader *feel* what you mean without telling them how to feel.

The Takeaway
Don't fear adjectives—train them.
When chosen well, they create precision, not clutter. When chosen badly, they bury the story in word mulch.
Keep the ones that matter, and cut the ones that don't. The difference between vivid and verbose is restraint.

Try This
Find three sentences in your current project that rely on adjectives for atmosphere.
Now, rewrite them once *without* the adjectives and once *with better ones*.
Which version makes you feel something? Which just fills space?
Keep the adjectives that deepen the moment—and let the rest fade quietly into revision history.

Adjectives are the drama queens of description—beautiful when they know their cues, unbearable when they don't. Used wisely, they color emotion and reveal texture. Used carelessly, they bury clarity under sequins and noise. The cure isn't abstinence; it's awareness. Choose your adjectives like jewels, not confetti, and your sentences will shine instead of shimmer themselves to death.

Adverb Overload—When Every Action Gets a Sidekick

Adverbs are like sidekicks who can't take a hint. They follow verbs everywhere, chirping commentary no one asked for. Used sparingly, they clarify action or tone. Used constantly, they make your prose feel like it's being narrated by a helicopter parent. The problem is that writers often use them to rescue weak verbs instead of strengthening the verbs themselves. This section is your intervention: a polite but firm reminder that not every action needs an emotional support word.

The Redundancy Problem

Instruction

Adverbs often arrive wearing capes, eager to save sentences that don't need saving. The trouble is, they usually repeat what the verb already says.

If you've ever written *"whispered quietly"* or *"shouted loudly,"* congratulations—you've fallen into the most common adverb trap of all.

Adverbs are meant to **add** meaning, not **echo** it. When they simply restate what the verb implies, they're not helping; they're hovering. Strong verbs don't need backup singers—they hit the note all by themselves.

Examples
No - *She whispered quietly.* → How else do you whisper?
Yes - *She whispered.*
No - *He nodded his head.* → What else would he nod—his spleen?

Yes - *He nodded.*
No - *The dog barked loudly.* → "Barked" already implies volume.
Yes - *The dog barked once, sharp and sudden.*
Yes - *She whispered urgently.* → Now we have *tone*, not repetition.
Yes - *The door creaked open slowly.* → The adverb controls *pacing*, not redundancy.

If an adverb repeats the verb's natural meaning, cut it.
If it changes or deepens the meaning, keep it.

The Takeaway
Adverbs are like seasoning—meant to enhance, not dominate.
When you catch one repeating what the verb already says, delete it with confidence.
The sentence won't collapse. It'll breathe.

Try This
Search your manuscript for words ending in *–ly*.
Now, for each one, ask:

- Does this adverb tell me something new?
- Or does it just repeat what the verb already made obvious?

Trim the echoes. Keep the nuance.
Your prose will sound cleaner—and your verbs will finally get to stand on their own two feet.

When They Actually Help

Instruction
Adverbs get a bad rap, but not all of them deserve exile. Some are genuinely useful—quiet little narrators that add precision or rhythm when a single verb can't carry the full emotional load.

The trick is to use adverbs that do one of three things:

1. **Change the meaning of the verb.** (*She spoke sharply* doesn't

mean the same as *She spoke.*)
2. **Control pacing or tone.** (*He exhaled slowly* feels different than *He exhaled.*)
3. **Create contrast or irony.** (*She laughed bitterly* adds flavor no synonym can replace.)

A well-placed adverb can shift the entire mood of a scene without breaking its flow. The key is intentionality—using adverbs for *effect*, not decoration.

Examples
Yes - *He answered softly, as if afraid the truth might shatter something.* → The adverb sets emotional tone.
Yes - *She opened the door carefully.* → Adds tension and pacing—useful in a suspenseful scene.
Yes - *They argued quietly in the kitchen.* → Creates intimacy and restraint, not redundancy.
Yes - *He almost smiled.* → "Almost" is pure precision—it changes the whole meaning.
No - *She completely finished the project.* → The adverb adds nothing. *Finished* already means *complete*.

Good adverbs fine-tune action; bad ones just stand there waving pom-poms. The difference is knowing whether the verb *needed* any further encouragement in the first place.

The Takeaway
A strong adverb is like a spotlight—used briefly, it draws attention where it's needed; left on too long, it blinds everyone.

Don't ban adverbs. Train them. The goal isn't *no adverbs*—it's *no lazy ones*.

Try This
Find five adverbs in your latest scene.
For each, test this rule:

- Does it **add** precision, emotion, or contrast?
- Or does it just **repeat** what the verb already implies?

Keep the ones that earn their keep.
Strike the rest.
Then read your scene aloud. You'll hear the difference—one version whispers; the other shouts.

The Lazy Verb Trap

Instruction

Adverbs love weak verbs—they're enablers. When a sentence leans too heavily on adverbs, it's usually because the verb isn't doing its job.

Instead of finding the right verb, writers toss in a generic one and dress it up: *walked slowly, said softly, looked quickly.* The result? A sentence that limps along when it could have sprinted.

Adverbs shouldn't be crutches for lazy verbs. They should be spotlights for strong ones.

If you find yourself reaching for an adverb, pause and ask: *Could I swap the verb for one that already contains that meaning?*

Examples
No - *She walked slowly across the room.*
Yes - *She crept across the room.*
No - *He said softly.*
Yes - *He murmured.*
No - *They looked quickly at each other.*
Yes - *They glanced at each other.*
No - *She ate hungrily.*
Yes - *She devoured the meal.*
Yes - *He whispered urgently.* → Adverb earns its keep because "urgently" adds emotion, not redundancy.

Each time you remove an adverb and replace the verb with a sharper one, your sentence gains muscle and loses bloat.

STEP AWAY FROM THAT SENTENCE 87

But here's the qualifier: sometimes, the softer phrasing is the right one—especially in dialogue or interior thought. Real people don't always "murmur" or "declare"; sometimes they just *say quietly*. Don't sacrifice natural rhythm for the sake of rule-following. Use precision where it matters most, and humanity everywhere else.

The Takeaway

If a verb needs an adverb to survive, it's not the right verb.

Use verbs that pull their own weight—they'll make your prose stronger, tighter, and more confident.

A good sentence doesn't *need* to be told how to feel. It already knows.

Try This

Do a "verb audit."

Pick one page of your manuscript and highlight every verb-adverb pair.

For each, ask:

- Can I replace this pair with one precise verb?
- If not, does the adverb change the meaning in a useful way?

Revise five sentences. Watch how your writing tightens instantly. That's not editing—that's evolution.

The –ly Epidemic

Instruction

There's nothing wrong with a little –ly now and then. It's a handy ending, tidy and efficient—until it multiplies. That's when your sentences start sounding like they were written by an overexcited sports commentator.

He quickly turned and loudly shouted before abruptly stopping.

See the problem? Too many –ly words make your prose sound breathless and overwrought. The issue isn't the suffix itself—it's the **overuse** of adverbs that rely on it to do the heavy lifting.

If your manuscript looks like it broke out in an –ly rash, it's time for triage.

Examples
No - *She suddenly realized she'd completely forgotten the utterly ridiculous meeting.*
Yes - *She realized she'd forgotten the ridiculous meeting.*
No - *He angrily slammed the door and stomped heavily away.*
Yes - *He slammed the door and stormed off.*
No - *The crowd loudly cheered as the hero bravely smiled and proudly waved.*
Yes - *The crowd erupted as the hero smiled and waved.*
Yes - *She quietly set down the cup.* → Here, the adverb adds tension; it's performing a job.
Yes - *He nearly missed the turn.* → "Nearly" changes the meaning, not the style.

The trick is to **differentiate between dependency and purpose**. If the –ly word exists because you couldn't find a stronger verb, it's a crutch.

If it adds timing, tone, or meaning, it's doing its job.

The Takeaway
Adverbs ending in –ly are the glitter of writing: a few can dazzle, but too many make a mess.

Before deleting them all in a fit of righteous minimalism, ask what each one contributes. If it's not pulling weight, sweep it out with the rest of the sparkle.

Try This
Open your manuscript and use your software's search function for "ly " (with a space after it).

Read each adverb aloud in its sentence.

Ask:

- Is this helping the reader *see* or *feel* something new?
- Or is it just padding the rhythm?

Delete the extras. Keep the essentials.
Your sentences will sound cleaner, sharper, and far more confident.

The Misplaced Adverb

Instruction

Adverbs are wanderers. They drift through sentences, looking for a home—and when they land in the wrong place, chaos follows. A misplaced adverb can quietly (and hilariously) change the meaning of a sentence.

Adverbs should sit as close as possible to the word they modify. When they don't, the reader's brain momentarily stumbles, trying to decide *who* or *what* is doing the action—and *how* they're doing it.

If your adverb can logically apply to more than one word in the sentence, it's probably misplaced.

Examples

No - *She almost drove her kids to school every day.* → Did she *almost drive* them, or did she drive them *almost every day*?

Yes - *She drove her kids to school almost every day.*

No - *He served the soup coldly to his guests.* → The soup wasn't cold—the *gesture* was.

Yes - *He coldly served the soup to his guests.*

No - *I only told him that he looked tired.* → "Only" is the slipperiest adverb in English; its placement changes everything.

Yes - *I told only him that he looked tired.* → Restricts *who* was told.

Yes - *I only told him that he looked tired.* → Restricts *what* was said (nothing more).

Yes - *I told him only that he looked tired.* → Same meaning, cleaner rhythm.

Yes - *She carefully opened the ancient book.* → Perfect placement—immediate clarity.

Adverbs are tiny but powerful. Where you put them determines *tone, rhythm,* and *meaning.* Treat them like explosives—handle with care.

The Takeaway

Word order isn't just grammar—it's choreography.

When an adverb slips out of position, it can trip the reader, confuse the action, or make your sentence say something you never intended. Keep your modifiers close to their partners, and no one will fall off the stage.

Try This

Take a paragraph of your writing and underline every adverb.

Now, for each one, draw an arrow to the word it's meant to modify—usually a **verb**, but sometimes an **adjective** or **another adverb**.

If that line crosses more than two other words, your adverb might be lost.

Reposition it for clarity.

Then read the sentence aloud—you'll hear it snap into place like puzzle pieces finally meeting.

What Adverbs Actually Modify

Instruction

Before you put your adverbs through the final test, it's worth remembering what they actually do. Adverbs are multitaskers—they don't just modify verbs. They also fine-tune **adjectives**, **other adverbs**, and sometimes **entire ideas**.

STEP AWAY FROM THAT SENTENCE

If adjectives describe *things*, adverbs describe *movement, manner,* and *modification*. They're the sentence's emotional and rhythmic control knobs, adjusting tone, timing, and intensity.

Examples
Yes - *He spoke quietly.* → Adverb modifying a **verb** (*how he spoke*).
Yes - *It's incredibly bright today.* → Adverb modifying an **adjective** (*how bright*).
Yes - *She moved very slowly.* → Adverb modifying another **adverb** (*how slowly*).
Yes - *Honestly, I don't care.* → Adverb modifying an **entire clause** (*the speaker's attitude*).

Adverbs are the great equalizers of expression—they reach across parts of speech to fine-tune meaning wherever it hides.

The Takeaway
Adjectives describe *nouns and pronouns*.
Adverbs describe *everything else*.

Use them with purpose, not panic—and remember, sometimes clarity needs a little calibration.

Try This
Write one sentence for each type of adverb use:

1. An adverb modifying a **verb** (*He laughed nervously.*)
2. An adverb modifying an **adjective** (*The tea was surprisingly good.*)
3. An adverb modifying another **adverb** (*She danced quite gracefully.*)
4. An adverb modifying an **entire clause** (*Frankly, it was chaos.*)

Then, swap or remove each adverb and reread the sentence.
Which ones changed the meaning? Which just changed the *mood*?
That's how you know who's really doing the work.

The Adverb Test

Instruction

After all this talk of trimming, training, and repositioning adverbs, it's time to test your instincts. Not every –ly word is evil, and not every cut makes your prose cleaner. The true skill lies in *knowing why* you're keeping or cutting an adverb.

Think of this as the final exam for modifier awareness. It's not about punishment—it's about precision.

An adverb earns its keep if it:

1. Changes or sharpens meaning (*She almost confessed.*)
2. Sets tone or emotion (*He spoke gently.*)
3. Adjusts timing or degree (*They barely survived.*)
4. Controls rhythm or pacing (*He hesitated briefly before replying.*)

If it doesn't do any of those things, it's probably excess decoration.

Examples

Yes - *She laughed nervously.* → The adverb deepens emotional context.

Yes - *He nodded slowly.* → Adds tension and visual rhythm.

No - *She whispered softly.* → Repeats what the verb already implies.

No - *He quickly sprinted away.* → "Sprinted" already includes "quickly."

Yes - *They nearly escaped.* → "Nearly" changes meaning—keep it.

An adverb that clarifies, sharpens, or surprises is doing real work.

One that simply repeats or softens meaning is just loitering in your syntax.

The Takeaway

The goal isn't to write without adverbs—it's to write without excuses.

Every adverb should justify its existence. If it can't, it's clutter.

When you master discernment, you'll stop fearing adverbs and start *wielding* them.

Try This

Choose a random paragraph from your manuscript.
For each adverb, apply the Adverb Test:

- Does it clarify *how, when, where,* or *to what extent* something happens?
- Does removing it weaken the meaning or just tidy the sentence?

Keep the ones that matter. Delete the ones that don't.
Then read both versions aloud.
If you can hear the difference—you've passed the test.

Adverbs aren't the enemy—they're just overenthusiastic. They show up uninvited, repeat what's already been said, and then insist they're helping. But when used deliberately, they can shape tone, tempo, and truth in ways no other part of speech can. The key is discernment: know when to keep them, when to cut them, and when to let them breathe. In the right hands, even an –ly can be lovely.

The Dangling Modifier Dilemma—When Descriptions Wander Off and Cause Trouble

A dangling modifier is a description that's lost its anchor—an orphaned phrase waving its arms, hoping someone will claim it. These poor modifiers start out with good intentions, but when they attach to the wrong word (or no word at all), the results range from confusing to comedic.

Writers rarely dangle modifiers on purpose. They happen when you describe something before naming *who* or *what* the description actually belongs to. The reader, ever cooperative, will try to make sense of it—and usually end up picturing a flying teacher, a talking sandwich, or a cat filing taxes.

This section will teach you how to keep your modifiers properly tethered—so your sentences stop dangling and start dazzling.

Spotting the Dangle

Instruction

A dangling modifier is a description that forgot what it was describing. It usually appears at the beginning of a sentence, eager to explain something—but without a clear subject to attach itself to. The result? A grammatical ghost, haunting a sentence that no longer makes sense.

Most dangling modifiers start innocently. A writer begins with an introductory phrase, then changes the rest of the sentence without adjusting the subject. What's left is a modifier waving desperately for attention—attached to the wrong noun or, worse, to none at all.

Examples

No - *Running through the forest, the trees blurred past.* → The trees weren't running. (At least, I hope not.)

Yes - *Running through the forest, I watched the trees blur past.*

No - *After reading the book, the movie seemed disappointing.* → The movie didn't read the book.

Yes - *After reading the book, I found the movie disappointing.*

No - *Covered in glitter, the editor sighed.* → (Okay, fine. Sometimes that one *is* accurate.)

Yes - *Covered in glitter, the manuscript sparkled under the desk lamp.*

Dangling modifiers often sound correct because our brains fill in the missing subject automatically. But readers can only interpret what's on the page—not what you *meant*.

The Takeaway

If a sentence opens with a descriptive phrase, the first noun after the comma should logically match it.

STEP AWAY FROM THAT SENTENCE

If it doesn't, you've got yourself a dangle.

Think of modifiers like leashes: if the noun isn't clearly holding the other end, the description has run off into the woods.

Try This

Take a few sentences from your own writing that begin with *-ing* phrases (*Walking down the street...*, *Looking out the window...*, etc.).

Then, ask:

- Who's actually doing the action in that opening phrase?
- Is that person or thing the first noun after the comma?

If not, rewrite it so the right subject takes the lead.

Example:

No - *Driving to work, the traffic annoyed me.*

Yes - *Driving to work, I was annoyed by the traffic.*

Congratulations—you've officially spotted your first wild dangle.

And now that you know how to find them, remember *why* it matters: clarity is trust. The moment a reader has to stop and sort out who's doing what, your story loses a bit of its magic. Keep your modifiers grounded, and your readers will follow wherever you lead.

> In 1762, Bishop Robert Lowth declared double negatives "ungrammatical," despite the fact that Chaucer, Shakespeare, and everyone else had been happily using them for centuries.

How to Fix a Dangling Modifier

Instruction

Now that you can spot a dangling modifier in the wild, it's time to learn how to catch and release it properly. Most danglers can be fixed with a small act of grammatical kindness: give them the subject they were looking for.

There are three main ways to untangle a dangle:

1. **Add the missing subject.**
2. **Rearrange the sentence so the modifier sits next to what it describes.**
3. **Rewrite the phrase entirely if it's just too awkward to save.**

Think of this as grammatical matchmaking—your modifier just needs to be reintroduced to the noun it was trying to describe all along.

Examples
Yes - Add the missing subject:
No - *While running down the street, the rain started.*
Yes - *While I was running down the street, the rain started.*
Yes - Rearrange the sentence:
No - *Glancing through the telescope, the planet came into view.*
Yes - *The planet came into view as I glanced through the telescope.*
Yes - Rewrite the phrase:
No - *After finishing the draft, the printer jammed.*
Yes - *After I finished the draft, the printer jammed.*
Yes - *The printer jammed right after I finished the draft.* (Cleaner, stronger.)

If it sounds like the wrong thing is doing the action—or like *no one* is doing the action—your modifier is still dangling. Keep revising until the logic lines up.

The Takeaway

STEP AWAY FROM THAT SENTENCE 97

Dangling modifiers aren't disasters; they're just lost causes looking for a home.

Give them a clear subject and a logical connection, and they'll behave beautifully.

If the fix feels clunky, simplify. Grammar should make your writing sound *smarter,* not *stiffer.*

Try This

1. Find three sentences in your current draft that begin with a descriptive phrase (*Running late,, Having finished,, Looking out the window,*).
2. Check: Who's actually performing the action?
3. Rewrite each sentence so the subject clearly matches the modifier.

Read them aloud. If they sound smooth and sensible, your modifier has been successfully rehomed.

The Misplaced Modifier Cousin

Instruction

Not all modifiers dangle. Some just wander off a little. A **misplaced modifier** is a description that's in the wrong spot—not completely unanchored, like a dangler, but sitting far enough away from the word it describes to cause confusion (or unintended comedy).

Unlike their dangling cousins, misplaced modifiers can be fixed without major surgery—just move them closer to what they modify. Think of it as herding adjectives and adverbs back to their rightful paddocks.

Examples

No - *She served sandwiches to the children on paper plates.* → The children were not, one hopes, on paper plates.

Yes - *She served sandwiches on paper plates to the children.*

No - *The detective discovered the suspect's fingerprints using a magnifying glass.* → The fingerprints didn't use the glass.

Yes - *Using a magnifying glass, the detective discovered the suspect's fingerprints.*

No - *She nearly ate a dozen cookies.* → Means she *almost* ate them, but stopped herself at the last minute.

Yes - *She ate nearly a dozen cookies.* → Corrects the placement and clarifies meaning.

No - *The dog chased the cat through the yard, barking loudly.* → Grammatically, "barking" might seem to modify "yard."

Yes - *Barking loudly, the dog chased the cat through the yard.*

Misplaced modifiers are sneaky because they *sound* fine at first glance. You have to listen for logic. If the sentence paints the wrong picture, the modifier's out of place.

The Takeaway

Modifiers are happiest when they're near what they describe.

If a sentence makes sense grammatically but creates a weird mental image, check for a misplacement. The cure is almost always the same: move the modifier closer to home.

Good writing is spatial awareness in sentence form.

Try This

Look for sentences that make you laugh—especially unintentionally.

Then ask:

- Is the modifier in the wrong place?
- Can you move it closer to the word or phrase it's describing?

Try rewriting three examples from your own work.

When the sentence sounds both clear and plausible, you've successfully corralled a wandering modifier.

Dangling and misplaced modifiers are the free spirits of grammar—always drifting, rarely landing where they should. They mean well, but left unchecked, they'll turn your prose into a circus of misplaced intent. The cure isn't fear; it's awareness. Keep your descriptions tethered to the right subjects, your modifiers close to their partners, and your sentences will stay upright and balanced. In the wild world of writing, even grammar's wanderers can be beautifully domesticated.

Stacking Modifiers—How Much Sparkle Is Too Much?

Modifiers are like spices—used thoughtfully, they create depth and flavor; used carelessly, they overwhelm the dish. By now, you know how to tame adjectives, rein in adverbs, and keep your modifiers from dangling. But what happens when you mix them all together?

Stacking modifiers is about **balance and hierarchy**—knowing which details should lead, which should follow, and when to stop seasoning the sentence. Too few modifiers, and the writing feels flat; too many, and it collapses under its own decoration. The goal isn't austerity—it's clarity that still shimmers.

This section explores how to layer modifiers with rhythm and intention so that your sentences shine with precision, not glitter with chaos.

Layering for Effect

Instruction

Layering modifiers is less about rules and more about rhythm. The question isn't *how many* modifiers you use—it's *how they work together*. A well-stacked sentence builds meaning in stages, guiding the reader through a clear visual or emotional progression.

The secret lies in **hierarchy**. Each modifier should earn its place by adding a new dimension of information—what kind, which one, how, when, or why. When you stack them without hierarchy, they all shout at once. When you stack them with intent, they sing in harmony.

Think of it like building a chord: the base note is your noun or verb; the modifiers are the harmonies. If they don't complement each other, you're just making noise.

Examples

Yes - *The old wooden bridge creaked softly in the mist.*

→ Each modifier builds logically: *old* (age), *wooden* (material), *softly* (sound), *in the mist* (setting). A full image, no clutter.

No - *The creaky, old, misty, wooden bridge softly, gently creaked.*

→ Every idea repeats another. We've lost rhythm and clarity.

Yes - *She spoke quickly but clearly, her voice trembling slightly.*

→ Different types of modifiers (adverbs + participial phrase) working together to shape pacing, tone, and emotion.

Yes - *Under the flickering streetlight, the tired detective leaned heavily against the cold, wet bricks.*

→ Layered modifiers create atmosphere and tone, yet the sentence still moves.

The Takeaway

Good layering is choreography.

Every modifier must enter in the right order, move with purpose, and leave space for the next.

If you can remove one without losing rhythm or meaning, it wasn't part of the dance.

Try This

Pick a vivid sentence from your manuscript and highlight every modifier it contains—adjectives, adverbs, phrases, and clauses.

Then ask:

1. Does each one add something new?

2. Are any just echoing what another already said?
3. Is the sentence still readable aloud without losing breath or focus?

Revise until your modifiers feel like harmony, not noise.

When your sentence reads like music instead of a marching band, you've mastered layering for effect.

The Adverb Cascade

Instruction

Adverbs are like confetti: one or two can make the moment sparkle, but too many and you've got a cleanup problem. They're small, harmless-looking words that pile up fast—each one promising to clarify, but together turning prose into quicksand.

An **adverb cascade** happens when writers keep adding "just one more" to fine-tune emotion or action:

He looked up suddenly, nervously, expectantly, hopefully.

The instinct is right—you're trying to be precise. The problem is that the more adverbs you stack, the less power each one holds. Instead of sharpening the image, you blur it into emotional static.

Examples

No - *She whispered softly, quietly, gently, lovingly into his ear.*

→ That's not whispering—it's a thesaurus malfunction.

Yes - *She whispered into his ear, her breath barely stirring the air.*

→ The image *shows* what the adverbs were trying to tell.

No - *He ran quickly, breathlessly, desperately down the hall.*

Yes - *He sprinted down the hall, breath ragged with panic.*

→ The stronger verb made the adverbs redundant.

No - *The dragon roared loudly.*

Yes - *The dragon roared.*

→ Dragons don't roar quietly.

The Takeaway

A cascade of adverbs doesn't add emotion—it dilutes it.

Use one if it changes meaning; delete it if it only repeats what the verb already implies.

When verbs do the heavy lifting, adverbs can take a well-earned nap.

Try This

Pick a paragraph from your work and underline every adverb (look for *-ly* endings first).

Then ask:

1. Does this adverb add something the verb doesn't already say?
2. Can I replace the verb with a stronger one instead?
3. If I remove it, does the sentence lose power—or gain focus?

Trim the ones that only echo.

When your prose stops tripping over its own modifiers, you've escaped the cascade.

The Adjective Avalanche

Instruction

Adjectives are the magpies of language—attracted to every shiny detail. They can add color, shape, texture, and mood to a noun, but too many at once bury it instead. When you stack them like mismatched ornaments, your reader gets lost in the clutter and forgets what the sentence was about in the first place.

An **adjective avalanche** happens when you try to describe everything at once: the look, the feel, the smell, the emotional tone, the lighting, and possibly the moral alignment of the object in question. The result is a noun gasping for air under all that description.

Your job as a writer isn't to tell readers everything about the thing—it's to choose *which* details help them see it best.

Examples

STEP AWAY FROM THAT SENTENCE 103

No - *The small, old, wooden, creaky, slightly leaning barn stood at the edge of the dark, weedy, overgrown field.*
→ That's not a barn; that's a filing system gone rogue.
Yes - *The old barn leaned at the edge of an overgrown field.*
→ Same scene, sharper focus, less breathlessness.
No - *Her long, silky, shimmering, honey-blonde hair fell over her delicate, pale, porcelain shoulders.*
→ Too many words fighting for attention, none of them winning.
Yes - *Her honey-blonde hair shimmered over her shoulders.*
→ Strong verb, fewer adjectives, same beauty—more power.
Yes - *The narrow, cobblestone street curved past shuttered windows and sleeping cats.*
→ Controlled, rhythmic, and atmospheric—this is how adjectives should dance, not collide.

The Takeaway
If you need more than two adjectives before a noun, stop and ask what you're really trying to say.
Choose the most revealing detail and let it carry the load.
Readers don't want a catalogue—they want a clear, memorable image.

Try This
Pick a paragraph with heavy description.

- Underline every adjective.
- Keep one that defines *what kind*, and one that suggests *mood or tone*.
- Delete the rest or convert them into verbs or sensory phrases.

Example:
No - *The cold, dark, lonely night sky hung above the silent, sleeping town.*
Yes - *The night sky hung above the sleeping town, vast and cold.*

When you can see the scene and still breathe while reading it, you've survived the avalanche.

When Layers Collapse

Instruction

Even the most elegant sentence can buckle under too much description. Pile modifiers too high, and meaning gets buried under the weight of its own adjectives. Readers can feel when a sentence is straining—when it stops sounding like voice and starts sounding like effort.

Collapsed layers happen when every detail shouts for equal attention. The writer forgets to choose what matters most. Without a visual or emotional focal point, the sentence stops feeling like a moment and starts reading like an inventory.

To keep your writing strong, aim for contrast: every modifier should either **sharpen** or **soften** the image, not repeat or compete. If a sentence feels bloated, trim until only the strongest descriptors remain.

Examples

No - *The long, winding, dusty, sun-baked road stretched endlessly before the weary, sweating, footsore traveler.*

→ Readers don't need a full weather report; they need an image that breathes.

Yes - *The dusty road stretched ahead, shimmering in the heat as the traveler trudged on.*

→ Same scene. Fewer words. Sharper impact.

No - *Her dark, silky, luxurious, shoulder-length hair framed her delicate, porcelain face beautifully.*

→ A tangle of description with nowhere for the eye to rest.

Yes - *Her dark hair framed her face, a quick gleam of light catching in the strands.*

→ One specific detail paints a stronger picture than six generic ones.

STEP AWAY FROM THAT SENTENCE

Yes - *He glanced at the broken sword—heavy, blood-stained, and still humming faintly with magic.*
→ Layered with purpose; each modifier adds new information or mood. This is the good kind of stacking.

The Takeaway
More is not always more.
If every modifier shines, none of them sparkle.
Stacking should build depth, not density. Choose your strongest details and let them carry the moment.

Try This
Take a paragraph from your work where you went all-in on description.

- Highlight every modifier.
- Circle the ones that create real sensory or emotional impact.
- Cross out the rest.

Now read it aloud.

If it feels lighter, smoother, and truer to your voice—you've just cleared the rubble and revealed the architecture underneath.

The Comma Clutter

Instruction

Commas are like traffic lights—useful when they guide the flow, infuriating when there are too many in one block. Modifier-heavy sentences tend to attract commas like magnets, until what was once clear becomes a slow crawl of pauses and potholes.

Comma clutter happens when writers try to cram every descriptive thought into one line, believing a few strategic commas will somehow make it all work. Spoiler: it won't. When a sentence has more commas than nouns, it's usually a cry for help.

A cluttered sentence doesn't just look messy—it *feels* messy. The rhythm stumbles, the pacing dies, and your reader starts gasping for air halfway through.

Examples

No - *The old, creaky, wooden, slightly crooked, somewhat haunted-looking door opened, slowly, with a long, shuddering groan, into the dark, chilly hallway.*

→ Somewhere in there is a decent image. It's just buried under punctuation rubble.

Yes - *The old door opened with a long, shuddering groan.*

→ The image is intact. The reader survives.

No - *She stepped carefully, quietly, almost reverently, through the narrow, twisting, overgrown path, her heart, somehow, both calm and racing.*

Yes - *She stepped quietly through the overgrown path, her heart both calm and racing.*

→ Every unnecessary comma is a speed bump. Remove them, and the sentence flows again.

Yes - *Under the flickering lantern light, the map looked alive, the ink shifting like spilled shadows.*

→ A few commas, used for rhythm, not repair. That's the sweet spot.

The Takeaway

Commas can't fix structural overload. If you're using them to hold your sentence together, the problem isn't punctuation—it's too many ideas fighting for space.

A good sentence breathes naturally; commas should enhance that rhythm, not interrupt it.

Try This

Take one of your longer sentences—especially one with five or more commas.

Read it out loud.

STEP AWAY FROM THAT SENTENCE

- Do you stumble?
- Lose track of the subject?
- Forget what the sentence was about halfway through?

Now, rewrite it as two sentences—or even three. You'll find the rhythm improves, and your reader will thank you with their continued attention.

How to Fix It

Instruction

After all the layering, cascading, avalanching, and cluttering, it's time to restore order. Fixing overstuffed modifier work isn't about purging all description—it's about choosing what deserves to stay.

The cure for modifier overload is **selective sparkle**. You're not stripping your writing of personality; you're giving every word a reason to exist. The strongest writers don't describe everything—they guide attention. They decide what glows and what fades quietly into the background.

Think of modifiers like light: one well-placed word can illuminate an image, but too many turn it blinding. The fix isn't restraint for restraint's sake—it's clarity in service of impact.

Examples

Yes - *The sea was calm, glassy, and endless.* → Three carefully chosen words; rhythm intact.

Yes - *Then the storm came, roaring like a god with something to prove.* → One vivid modifier carries the emotion.

No - *The sea was calm, shimmering, silver-blue, quietly vast, and hauntingly endless.* → Every synonym fighting for screen time.

Yes - *He smiled—a slow, reluctant thing that softened the edges of his anger.* → Focused, intentional, evocative.

Yes - *The candle flickered once, then died.* → No modifiers needed. The image burns clean.

The Takeaway
Good writing doesn't sparkle everywhere—it **strategically glows**.
Let a few moments shine so the rest can breathe.
Readers remember contrast, not clutter. When every line tries to be beautiful, none of them are.
Try This

1. Pick a descriptive paragraph you love—but suspect might be overworked.
2. Highlight one sentence that deserves to shine—the emotional or visual centerpiece.
3. Polish *that* sentence with precision.
4. Then strip the others back to simplicity.

Read it aloud.
If the key moment gleams against quieter prose, you've fixed it.
That's how you end the avalanche, silence the cascade, and let your writing glow—deliberately, confidently, and just enough to leave an afterimage.

Every writer goes through a modifier phase—the glorious, adjective-adorned, adverb-infested era when every sentence feels unfinished without a flourish. But mastery isn't in adding polish; it's in knowing when the page already shines. You've learned how to stack, trim, balance, and breathe—how to build rhythm instead of rubble. When you control your modifiers, you control the reader's focus.

So, stack wisely. Let a few sentences shimmer while the rest stay steady. The real sparkle of language isn't in decoration—it's in design.

Connectors: Prepositions & Conjunctions

Every sentence is a social gathering of words, and someone has to make the introductions. Enter the connectors—the prepositions and conjunctions that keep conversation flowing and prevent nouns and verbs from bumping into each other awkwardly at the grammar party.

Prepositions tell us **where, when, and how** things relate: above, beyond, under, inside, beside, before.

Conjunctions tell us **how ideas connect**: and, but, or, because, although.

They're the duct tape of language—usually invisible, absolutely essential, and occasionally applied upside down.

Preposition Purgatory

Prepositions get a bad rap for being small, confusing, and impossible to memorize. They sneak into sentences, make everything sound right, and then betray you when you least expect it. (Ask anyone who's ever argued about being "on the bus" vs. "in the bus.")

But without them, English would collapse into chaos. Prepositions tell your reader where ideas live in space and time—and occasionally in the emotional void between "over it" and "into it."

Ending with a Preposition (Totally Fine, Usually)

Once upon a time, teachers insisted that ending a sentence with a preposition was a moral failing. "A preposition," they said, "is not something to end a sentence with." And we were left wondering, "Are you sure?"

Ironically, that rule was imported from Latin—a language that doesn't even use prepositions the same way English does.

Modern grammar calls that nonsense. In English, a preposition at the end of a sentence is not a crime—it's a choice for clarity or rhythm. "That's the book I told you about" sounds natural. "That's the book about which I told you" sounds like you swallowed a Victorian etiquette manual.

Instruction

A preposition may appear at the end of a sentence when moving it would make the sentence awkward or unnatural.

If the object of the preposition is clear and the sentence flows smoothly, you're fine.

Examples:

Yes - What are you waiting for?

Yes - That's the hill I'll die on.

No - On what are you waiting? (Technically correct; emotionally dead.)

The Takeaway

Don't contort your sentences to satisfy a ghost rule.

If a preposition sounds better at the end, leave it there. Grammar exists to serve clarity, not impress a long-dead Latin scholar.

Try This

Rewrite these sentences to sound natural, ending with a preposition when it feels right:

1. That's the chair **on which** I was sitting.
2. The project is something **about which** I'm excited.
3. This is the person **with whom** I was speaking.

Now read both versions aloud. If the "correct" one makes you cringe, congratulations—you speak modern English.

Idiomatic Minefields (on / in / at)

English prepositions are less rules than vibes. You're **on** a train but **in** a car. You meet **at** the corner but stand **on** the corner. None of it is logical; all of it is idiomatic—meaning we just say it that way because generations before us did.

Instruction

Some prepositions form fixed partnerships with certain nouns, verbs, or adjectives. These combinations are called *idiomatic expressions*. They don't always translate logically, and swapping them can make your sentence sound foreign or off-kilter.

Common patterns:

- **At** = a specific point (time or place) → at noon, at the corner, at home
- **In** = enclosure or larger area → in the city, in a car, in Canada
- **On** = surface or connected platform → on the table, on a trip, on Monday

There are hundreds of exceptions, and arguing with them is like yelling at gravity.

The Takeaway

Prepositions are learned by pattern, not logic. If you're ever unsure, listen for what native speakers say or check a reliable usage guide.

And remember: sounding natural beats sounding mechanical. You live **in** a house, not **at** a house; you sit **on** a chair, not **in** it (unless you're tiny or dramatic).

Try This

Choose the correct preposition:

1. We arrived ___ the airport just ___ time.
2. She's ___ the bus heading ___ downtown.
3. I'll see you ___ Monday ___ the café ___ the corner.

Then, make up your own three-sentence mini-scene that uses *on*, *in*, and *at* naturally. If it reads smoothly, you're winning.

Between You and Me

Here's where grammar and ego collide. People think "between you and I" sounds elegant. It doesn't. It sounds like someone dressed *me* up in *I's* clothes and hoped no one would notice.

Instruction

Use *me*, not *I*, after prepositions like *between*, *to*, *for*, or *with*. That's because prepositions always take objects, not subjects.
Examples:
Yes - Between you and me, this meeting could've been an email.
No - Between you and I, this meeting could've been an email.
Yes - She sat beside him and me.
No - She sat beside he and I.

The Takeaway

Formality doesn't mean correctness. "Between you and I" is a grammatical imposter—it snuck in because people wanted to sound polite. True polish is accuracy wrapped in ease.

Try This

Fix these sentences:

1. The decision was made by the director and I.
2. That secret stays between you and I.
3. The teacher gave extra credit to Sarah and I.

Then write one of your own using *me* after a preposition. Bonus points if it's a confession worth keeping "between you and me."

Prepositions may look small, but they pull a lot of weight. Misplace one, and your meaning goes flying off in the wrong direction. Keep them grounded, purposeful, and true to their relationships—like loyal little word matchmakers. Between you and me, it's never the size of the word that matters—it's how precisely you place it.

> The word *of* used to do the job of *from*. That's why we still say *"made of clay"* instead of *"made from clay."* You're speaking with linguistic fossils.

Conjunction Confusion

If prepositions are the matchmakers of grammar, conjunctions are the party planners. They decide who gets to sit together and which ideas are allowed to mingle. Without them, every sentence would be a lonely island.

Conjunctions link words, phrases, and clauses—sometimes gently, sometimes recklessly. Done right, they create rhythm and clarity. Done wrong, they produce run-ons, fragments, and chaos.

FANBOYS Done Right

For, And, Nor, But, Or, Yet, So—the seven coordinating conjunctions holding English together with pure stubbornness. Collectively, they're known as **FANBOYS**, and they connect equals: word to word, phrase to phrase, clause to clause.

Instruction

Use a comma before a coordinating conjunction when it joins two independent clauses (each could stand alone as a sentence).

Examples:
Yes - The dragon yawned, **and** smoke filled the room.
Yes - She wanted to stay, **but** her nerves disagreed.
No - The dragon yawned and smoke filled the room.
Note:
If the clauses are **short and clearly related**, some writers omit the comma. For example:
He ran and she hid.

That's acceptable in informal writing or fiction, but the comma is always correct—and preferred for clarity in professional or academic work.

Don't start a sentence with *but* or *and*? No longer a thing to worry about. Both are perfectly acceptable—especially in modern writing where rhythm and tone matter more than dusty prohibitions.

The Takeaway
FANBOYS aren't there to restrain you; they're there to balance you.
If the parts are equal, connect them confidently.
If you start a sentence with one, do it for style, not rebellion.

Try This
Combine these pairs correctly:

1. The rain poured. The concert continued.
2. He didn't study. He still aced the test.
3. I could stay home. I could face my destiny.

Now, start three new sentences with *But*, *And*, or *So*—make them bold, make them musical, and watch how they change tone.

> "And" is one of the oldest words in the English language—so old it predates English itself. Its ancestor appeared in the earliest Germanic tongues, linking ideas long before anyone called it grammar.

Subordination for Clarity

Not all ideas deserve equal billing. Sometimes one needs to take the spotlight while another quietly provides context. That's where **subordinating conjunctions**—words like *because, although, when, if, since, while*—step in.

Instruction

A subordinating conjunction links a dependent clause (incomplete thought) to an independent clause (complete thought).

Examples:

Yes - Because the dragon was tired, she napped on the castle roof.

Yes - She napped on the castle roof **because** she was tired.

No - Because she was tired. (That's a fragment crying for closure.)

Punctuation tip: if the dependent clause comes first, add a comma. If it comes second, skip it.

Dialogue note:

Fragments like *"Because she was tired."* are fair game in dialogue. Characters are allowed to be dramatic, tired, or mid-tantrum. Grammar takes a back seat when it's serving voice and realism—and sometimes the sentence just doesn't feel like finishing itself.

The Takeaway
Subordination is grammar's way of showing hierarchy.
It tells readers which idea matters most and keeps sentences from fighting for attention.
Use it to clarify cause, contrast, or condition—not to overcomplicate.

Try This
Complete each with a subordinating conjunction of your choice:

1. _____ the knight arrived, the feast had already begun.
2. The villagers fled _____ they saw smoke.
3. She smiled _____ her heart was breaking.

Now, write one long sentence that uses both a coordinating and a subordinating conjunction. Then rewrite it shorter. Notice how structure changes emphasis.

Oxford Comma: Crimes & Misdemeanors

The Oxford comma—that final comma before *and* in a list—is the bane of many an editor' existence. Some call it unnecessary; others call it civilization.

Instruction
The Oxford (or serial) comma appears before the final *and* or *or* in a series of three or more items.
Example:
Yes - I dedicated this book to my parents, Harpur, and the dragon.
Without it: I dedicated this book to my parents, Harpur and the dragon. (Suddenly my parents *are* Harpur and the dragon.)
Use it consistently—especially in anything formal, published, or legally binding. Entire lawsuits have hinged on its absence.

The Takeaway

STEP AWAY FROM THAT SENTENCE

The Oxford comma prevents chaos and family drama. Use it unless your style guide forbids it—and even then, use it quietly and deny everything.

Try This
Punctuate these sentences with and without the Oxford comma. Which reads more clearly?

1. I love my editor, coffee and peace and quiet.
2. She left her inheritance to her cats, her friends and a local haunted manor.
3. We bought apples, pears, and dragons.

Now write one sentence where omitting the Oxford comma causes delicious confusion.

Connectors are the unsung heroes of syntax—tiny, tireless words that keep your sentences from collapsing into word salad. Prepositions give your ideas location and logic; conjunctions give them relationships and rhythm.

Use them with intent: end with a preposition when it sounds human, pick the idiom that fits, give *me* its rightful place after *between*, and let your conjunctions guide the dance without stepping on anyone's toes.

The goal isn't perfection—it's flow. When your connectors do their job right, the reader doesn't even notice them. They just feel the current of your thought carrying them effortlessly from one idea to the next.

Sentences & Structure (CSI—Syntax)

Welcome to the scene of the syntax.

This is where words stop being individuals and start forming organized crime rings called *sentences*. Every clause has a motive, every comma knows too much, and your job—as the forensic grammarian—is to figure out who connects to whom, and why the punctuation looks guilty.

Sentence structure is the skeleton of your writing. It holds everything upright, but when a bone breaks—or multiplies into an unnatural run-on—things start to limp. This section will show you how to keep your sentences standing tall: balanced, breathable, and beautifully readable.

From fragments that don't know when to grow up, to run-ons that never shut up, we'll dissect the usual suspects and teach you how to write with rhythm and intention.

Because when syntax sings, the story moves.

Fragment Frenzy (and the Stylish Fragment)

Once upon a time, a teacher told you every sentence needs a subject and a verb.

They were right.

Mostly.

A fragment is what happens when a sentence goes rogue—missing its subject, verb, or complete thought. It's the grammatical equivalent of someone trailing off mid-story: *If only I had known...*

But here's the twist: not all fragments are bad. Some are **stylish**—intentional breaks in the rhythm that make your writing sound alive, conversational, or dramatic. The trick is knowing when you're bending the rule and when you've just dropped the ball.

Instruction

STEP AWAY FROM THAT SENTENCE

A complete sentence contains **a subject (who/what)** and **a predicate (what they do or are)**—a complete idea.

A **fragment** lacks one of these essential pieces or fails to stand alone logically.

Examples (accidental):
No - Because the dragon was tired. (incomplete—waiting for the main clause)
No - When we arrived at the castle. (same problem)
Fixed:
Yes - The dragon was tired.
Yes - The castle loomed before us.

But when used *deliberately*, fragments can create rhythm or emphasis:
Yes - And then—silence.
Yes - No warning. No mercy.
Yes - A single spark.

Intentional fragments work because the reader feels what's missing. The pause carries meaning.

Quick test: if a fragment feels like a *choice*, it's style.
If it feels like a *typo*, it's trouble.

The Takeaway

Fragments are the sentence world's rebels. Used well, they add punch, pacing, and intimacy. Used poorly, they make you sound like you lost your train of thought.

When revising, ask yourself:

- Did I mean for this to be incomplete?
- Does it flow naturally from what came before?
  If yes, keep it. If no, connect it.

Try This

1. Write three intentional fragments that create tension or

emotion.

(*Example: Too late. Too high. Too far to turn back.*)
2. Find one unintentional fragment in your own writing and fix it.
3. Rewrite this paragraph into a single complete sentence:

When the storm began. The candles flickered. Shadows trembled. Then rewrite it *back* into fragments—this time for drama.

> The conjunction "because" was once two words: "by cause." So next time someone tells you you're wrong, you can say, "By cause, I know what I'm talking about."

Run-On Rampage (Coordination vs. Punctuation)

Ah, the run-on sentence—grammar's version of a freeway pileup. Words speeding in every direction, clauses merging without signals, and somewhere in the wreckage, a poor comma trying to hold it all together.

Run-ons don't happen because you wrote too much; they happen because you didn't connect ideas correctly. Coordination and punctuation are what keep your sentences from crashing.

Instruction

STEP AWAY FROM THAT SENTENCE

A **run-on sentence** (or *fused sentence*) happens when two or more independent clauses are jammed together without the proper link or punctuation.

Wrong:
No - The dragon roared the villagers screamed everyone hid.
Right:
Yes - The dragon roared, **and** the villagers screamed.
Yes - The dragon roared; the villagers screamed.
Yes - The dragon roared. The villagers screamed.
There are two main ways to fix a run-on:

1. **Coordination** – join clauses with a comma and a coordinating conjunction (FANBOYS: *for, and, nor, but, or, yet, so*).
   - The knight raised his sword, **but** his knees betrayed him.
2. **Punctuation** – use a semicolon or a period to separate complete ideas.
   - The wizard blinked; the spell fizzled.
   - The wizard blinked. The spell fizzled.

Comma splices are the run-on's cousin—when two independent clauses are joined by just a comma.
No - The dragon woke, the castle trembled.
Yes - The dragon woke, **and** the castle trembled.
Yes - The dragon woke; the castle trembled.

Remember: commas can't hold up full sentences by themselves. They're connectors, not welders.

The Takeaway
Run-ons aren't about length—they're about logic. You can write a hundred-word sentence that's perfectly correct if the clauses are properly connected, or a ten-word sentence that's a total disaster if they aren't.

When in doubt, look for where you could naturally take a breath or place a period. If your sentence keeps talking after the thought's already done, you're probably on a rampage.

Try This

1. Fix these run-ons three different ways (conjunction, semicolon, period):
   - The dragon fell asleep the villagers finally relaxed.
   - He wanted to run he couldn't find his shoes.
2. Write one intentionally ridiculous run-on, then repair it without losing its energy.
   (Example: The knight ran into the forest he tripped over a root he swore vengeance on trees forever → The knight ran into the forest, tripped over a root, and swore vengeance on trees forever.)
3. Challenge: Write a single long sentence—at least 40 words—that's grammatically correct. Use proper coordination and punctuation. If it still reads smoothly, you've achieved syntactical hero status.

Comma Splice Crisis (How to Spot/Fix)

A comma splice looks harmless. Just a tiny mark, a polite pause. But left unchecked, it's the silent killer of clarity—sneaking between independent clauses that deserve their own space and pretending everything's fine. Spoiler: it's not.

Comma splices are what happen when two complete sentences are joined by only a comma. It's like connecting two houses with a garden hose and calling it plumbing.

Instruction

A **comma splice** joins two independent clauses (each with its own subject and verb) using only a comma, with no conjunction or proper punctuation.

Examples (wrong):

STEP AWAY FROM THAT SENTENCE 123

No - The dragon yawned, the villagers fled.
No - He promised to edit the chapter, he forgot immediately.
Correct options:
Yes - Add a **coordinating conjunction**: The dragon yawned, **and** the villagers fled.
Yes - Use a **semicolon**: The dragon yawned; the villagers fled.
Yes - Split it into **two sentences**: The dragon yawned. The villagers fled.
Yes - Use a **subordinator**: When the dragon yawned, the villagers fled.
Each fix changes the rhythm slightly—pick the one that fits your tone.
Quick test: Read your sentence aloud. If you naturally pause longer than a comma's worth of breath, you probably need stronger punctuation.
The Takeaway
Commas are for connection, not containment. When you ask one to hold up two full sentences, it collapses under the weight.
Think of punctuation as architecture:

- **Commas** are doors—quick transitions.
- **Semicolons** are hallways—smooth links between rooms.
- **Periods** are walls—clean separations.

If your clauses each deserve their own address, give them proper real estate.
Try This

1. Fix the comma splices below in at least two different ways each:
    - She opened the manuscript, the edits stared back at her.
    - The storm passed, the air smelled like relief.

- He hit "send," instant regret followed.
2. Write your own comma splice, then fix it three ways. Notice how punctuation changes tone and pacing.
3. Bonus challenge: Find a page in your current project and check for comma splices. You might be shocked at how many polite little disasters are hiding in plain sight.

Parallel Parking (Lists, Comparisons, Correlative Pairs)

Parallel structure is grammar's version of choreography. Every phrase has to move in sync, or the whole sentence starts tripping over itself. When words are meant to match—whether in a list, a comparison, or a correlative pair—they need to be balanced.

Think of it like assembling a band: if everyone's playing the same song but in different keys, you don't have music—you have chaos.

Instruction

Parallel structure (also called *parallelism*) means using the same grammatical form for ideas that belong together. It gives writing rhythm, clarity, and style.

You use parallelism most often in three places:

1. **Lists**
   Yes - She likes **reading, writing,** and **editing**.
   No - She likes **to read, writing,** and **editing**. (Inconsistent forms.)
2. **Comparisons**
   Yes - Harpur is braver **than Arthur is careful**.
   No - Harpur is braver **than Arthur cares about safety**. (Mismatched structure.)
3. **Correlative pairs** (either/or, neither/nor, both/and, not only/but also)
   Yes - He wanted **not only** to win **but also** to learn.

No - He wanted **not only** to win **but also** learning from it.

Quick test:
If your list or pair reads like it's limping, check for mismatched grammar. Each item should plug into the same sentence frame cleanly.

The Takeaway
Parallelism isn't just correctness—it's rhythm. When similar ideas are expressed in similar ways, readers glide instead of stumble.

Uneven structure is like hitting a pothole mid-sentence: the meaning's still there, but the ride's rough.

As you revise, listen to your sentences. Balanced ones hum; unbalanced ones hiccup.

Try This

1. Fix the parallelism in these sentences:
   - She wanted to laugh, to cry, and dancing.
   - The hero promised to save the kingdom, defeat the villain, and that he'd call his mother.
   - The editor was precise, patient, and with no sense of humor.
2. Write one sentence with a parallel list, one with a parallel comparison, and one with a correlative pair.
3. Bonus challenge: find a paragraph from your writing and check for balance. Could you make the rhythm smoother just by aligning the structures? (Hint: probably yes.)

The Clause Clause (Independent, Dependent, Restrictive, Nonrestrictive)

Clauses are the true power brokers of grammar. They decide who gets to stand alone, who must be escorted, and who interrupts the sentence just to show off. If words are the workers and phrases are the departments, clauses are upper management—running the whole operation while pretending they're underpaid.

Understanding how clauses connect (and when they shouldn't) is the key to mastering sentence structure. Once you know who's independent and who's not, your writing stops sounding accidental and starts sounding intentional.

Instruction

A **clause** is a group of words with a subject and a verb.

It can be either **independent** (a full sentence) or **dependent** (needs backup).

Independent clause:
Yes - The dragon snored.
(It's a complete thought—a self-sufficient sentence.)

Dependent clause:
No - Because the dragon snored.
(That's just a teaser. It needs another clause to finish the thought.)

Combine them:
Yes - Because the dragon snored, everyone hid under the bed.

Restrictive vs. Nonrestrictive Clauses

These describe how extra information behaves:

- **Restrictive clause**—*essential* to meaning. No commas.
  Yes - The knight **who wore the purple cape** won the duel.
  (We need that clause to know *which* knight.)
- **Nonrestrictive clause**—*extra* information. Set off with commas.
  Yes - The knight, **who wore the purple cape**, won the duel.
  (We already know which knight; the clause just adds flair.)

Quick test: If you can remove the clause without changing the sentence's core meaning, it's nonrestrictive—and needs commas.

The Takeaway

STEP AWAY FROM THAT SENTENCE

Clauses are the glue that hold sentences together, but you have to know which type of glue you're using.

Independent clauses can stand alone. Dependent ones can't.

Restrictive clauses define; nonrestrictive ones decorate.

Get this balance right, and your writing feels confident and polished. Get it wrong, and your sentences start sticking to things they shouldn't.

Try This

1. Label each clause as **independent** or **dependent**:
   - When the sun rose.
   - The villagers cheered.
   - Because the dragon was gone.
   - They rebuilt the walls.
2. Decide whether these need commas:
   - The manuscript that you edited won an award.
   - My editor who lives in Canada is a genius.
   - My editor, who lives in Canada, is a genius.
3. Write one sentence with each:
   - Independent + Dependent
   - Restrictive
   - Nonrestrictive
4. Bonus challenge: Write one sentence that contains *all four* clause types. (Yes, it's possible. Just don't blame me if it gets... clause-trophobic.)

> Medieval scribes wrote sentences with no punctuation and no spaces. Readers had to figure it out by breathing in the right places.

Sentence Variety: Rhythm & Flow (Length, Cadence, Breath)

Every writer has a rhythm. You can hear it if you read your work aloud—that rise and fall, that pulse of language that either keeps a reader hooked or puts them gently to sleep. Sentence structure isn't just about correctness; it's about **music**.

Too many short sentences, and your prose feels choppy.

Too many long ones, and it starts to drown in its own syntax.

The secret is variety—like alternating drumbeats, each one creating contrast, tension, and relief.

Instruction

Sentence variety means deliberately mixing sentence **length**, **structure**, and **rhythm** to control pacing and emotion.

1. Length

Short sentences punch. Long sentences pull. Both are tools.

- Short: The dragon blinked.
- Long: The dragon blinked once, slowly, as if weighing the cost of another century's sleep before deciding the world could manage without him.

STEP AWAY FROM THAT SENTENCE

2. Structure
Vary your clauses and connectors. Mix simple, compound, complex, and compound–complex forms.

- Simple: The knight ran.
- Compound: The knight ran, and the dragon followed.
- Complex: When the knight ran, the dragon followed.
- Compound–complex: When the knight ran, the dragon followed, and everyone regretted everything.

3. Rhythm
Punctuation creates breath. Use it like a conductor uses tempo. Commas soften. Periods stop. Semicolons glide.
You can even bend rhythm through repetition:

- *He ran. He stumbled. He fell. He rose.* (staccato urgency)
- *He ran, stumbling, falling, rising—relentless.* (lyrical drive)

Read your sentences out loud. If you run out of breath, cut. If you sound like a telegram, lengthen.

Note:
This isn't a free pass to stack adverbs or modifiers—it's about **controlling rhythm**, not cluttering it. The goal is musical movement, not grammatical overkill.

The Takeaway
Good writing moves like a living thing—inhale, exhale, sprint, rest.
Vary your sentence lengths the way a composer varies notes: each choice affects tone and energy.
Monotony kills rhythm. Variety revives it.
When in doubt, treat your prose like music and edit by ear.

Try This

1. Take a paragraph you've written. Mark each sentence as

short, **medium**, or **long**. If you see a pattern (all short or all long), rewrite one or two for contrast.
2. Write three sentences describing a thunderstorm—one short and sharp, one long and flowing, one balanced in between. Read them aloud. Feel the change in pacing.
3. Bonus challenge: Craft one paragraph that starts calm, builds momentum, and ends in a single, clipped sentence. That's rhythm control—grammar's version of a mic drop.

You've now seen what really happens at the scene of the syntax: fragments that break free, run-ons that overstay their welcome, clauses that squabble over commas, and rhythm that can make or break a page.

Sentence structure is where grammar becomes style. It's not just about correctness; it's about **control**. Knowing when to stop, when to flow, and when to let silence do the talking.

If you treat every sentence as a living thing—with bones, breath, and heartbeat—you'll start to feel the difference between writing that merely functions and writing that moves.

So keep your syntax clean, your rhythm intentional, and your commas honest.

Because when structure works, readers don't notice it. They just keep reading.

Agreement & Logic (Play Nice)

If sentences are relationships, agreement is therapy.

Every word has to know who it's talking about, what it's referring to, and whether it's singular, plural, or having an identity crisis. The moment one partner stops agreeing with the other—boom—your sentence files for grammatical divorce.

Agreement keeps grammar civil. It's the difference between *the team are fighting* and *the team is fighting*, between *everyone brought their lunch* and *everyone brought his lunch* (and the collective groan that follows).

This section is where we make sure every part of your sentence plays nicely: subjects with verbs, pronouns with antecedents, logic with itself. Because when agreement breaks down, even beautiful prose starts sounding like a bad meeting transcript.

Agreement Anxiety (Subject–Verb Agreement; Indefinite Pronouns)

Subject–verb agreement is grammar's most basic courtesy: if the subject is singular, the verb should be too; if the subject is plural, the verb should follow suit. Simple enough—until English starts playing dress-up and sending in decoys like *everyone, none,* and *the committee.* Then things get twitchy.

Agreement mistakes don't happen because writers are lazy; they happen because English is a shapeshifter. Sometimes a singular word looks plural (*news*), and sometimes a plural idea acts singular (*mathematics*). No wonder everyone's anxious.

Instruction

At its core, **agreement** means that a verb must match its subject in **number** (singular/plural) and **person** (first/second/third).

Basic rules:

Yes - The dragon **sleeps**. (singular subject → singular verb)
Yes - The dragons **sleep**. (plural subject → plural verb)
The confusion starts with **tricky subjects**:

1. **Prepositional distractions**
    - The pile **of manuscripts** *is* enormous. (The subject is *pile*, not *manuscripts*.)
2. **Collective nouns**
    - The team *is* winning. (as a single unit)
    - The team *are* arguing among themselves. (as individuals—more common in British English)
3. **Indefinite pronouns** (everyone, each, neither, someone, anybody, etc.)
    - These are **singular**, even when they sound plural:
    Yes - Everyone **loves** a dragon story.
    No - Everyone **love** a dragon story.
4. **Either/or & neither/nor** constructions

The verb agrees with the subject **closest to it**:
No - Everyone **love** a dragon story.
Either the knights **or the dragon is** lying.
Yes - Either the dragon **or the knights are** lying.
Quick test: Find your true subject—ignore the prepositional fluff. Then check if it's one thing or more than one thing. Match the verb accordingly.

The Takeaway

Agreement errors break reader trust the way bad harmonies ruin a song. When the subject and verb don't move together, the rhythm of the sentence falls apart.

Always check who's actually doing the action. Words that come between the subject and verb often cause the trouble. Agreement isn't about rules—it's about clarity. Your reader shouldn't have to pause to mentally edit your verb.

STEP AWAY FROM THAT SENTENCE 133

Try This

1. Fix the agreement in these sentences:
   - The list of supplies *include* parchment and ink.
   - Everyone *know* the meeting was today.
   - Either the editor or the authors *is* confused.
   - The data *shows* several inconsistencies. (Trick: *data* is plural in formal use, but singular in casual English—choose your audience.)
2. Write one sentence with a collective noun, one with an indefinite pronoun, and one with a compound subject joined by *and*. Make sure each verb agrees naturally.
3. Bonus challenge: Write one grammatically correct sentence that could *sound* wrong at first glance (like "Mathematics is hard"), and explain why it's right.

Either/Neither/Nor/Nonsense (Closest-to-Verb Rule, Traps)

Few grammar rules cause more confusion—or more arguments—than deciding whether to say *is* or *are* after *either/or* or *neither/nor*. It's like trying to pick a side in a family feud where both are technically right, depending on who speaks last.

The truth? English plays favorites. The verb agrees with whichever subject is **closest** to it. That's the law of proximity, and it's surprisingly democratic—if a little chaotic.

Instruction

When you have two subjects joined by **either/or** or **neither/nor**, your verb must agree with the one nearest it.

Examples:
Yes - Either the knights **or the dragon is** lying.
Yes - Either the dragon **or the knights are** lying.
Yes - Neither the editor **nor the authors were** pleased.

If one subject is singular and the other plural, put the plural one second whenever possible—it sounds more natural:

Yes - Either the wizard or the apprentices **are** responsible.

No - Either the apprentices or the wizard **is** responsible. (Technically correct but awkward.)

Beware the double trap:

Writers often forget the *nor* half of *neither/nor* and use *or* instead—mixing signals. Keep them in pairs:

- Either/or (positive or neutral options)
- Neither/nor (negative or excluding options)

Bonus chaos:

When a sentence begins with *either/neither of + plural noun*, it's **singular** in formal writing but can lean plural in informal use:

Yes - Neither of the dragons **is** friendly. (formal)

Yes - Neither of the dragons **are** friendly. (acceptable in modern casual style)

Pick a lane and stay consistent within your manuscript's tone.

The Takeaway

Grammar's proximity rule is one of its more reasonable quirks: the verb agrees with the noun right beside it.

So if the closest subject is singular, use a singular verb; if it's plural, use plural. And when in doubt, reorder the sentence to make it sound like something an actual human would say.

Consistency trumps technicality. Your goal isn't to impress grammarians—it's to make meaning seamless.

Try This

1. Fill in the correct verb form:
    - Either the author or the editors ___ to blame.
    - Neither the dragons nor the knight ___ ready for battle.

- Either the map or the directions ___ wrong.
- Neither of the essays ___ finished.

2. Rewrite one sentence so that it *changes* from singular to plural agreement—then explain how moving the subjects around affected the verb.
3. Bonus challenge: Write one sentence that looks wrong but isn't, using both *either/or* and *neither/nor*. Make it funny if you can—grammar needs a sense of humor too.

Double Negative Drama (Standard vs. Rhetorical Style)

Ah, the double negative: English's moody teenager. Always misunderstood, sometimes rebellious, occasionally poetic.

In standard grammar, two negatives cancel each other out. *I don't need no help* literally means *I do need help*. But in rhetorical or regional English, double negatives can be intentional—used for emphasis, rhythm, or voice. The trick is knowing when it's character... and when it's chaos.

Instruction

A **double negative** occurs when two negative words appear in the same clause, unintentionally reversing the meaning:

No - I don't have no pencils. → technically means "I do have pencils."

Yes - I don't have **any** pencils.

Common negative words: *no, not, never, nothing, nobody, none, hardly, scarcely, barely.*

In standard English:

One negative per clause is plenty. Add more and you risk confusing readers—or making your narrator sound uneducated unless that's your goal.

In rhetorical or stylistic English:

Writers sometimes use double negatives deliberately for tone or authenticity:

Yes - *I can't get no satisfaction.* (colloquial, poetic, iconic)

Yes - *He wasn't no fool.* (dialect, attitude, character voice)

Editorial note:

In fiction, double negatives can convey realism or rhythm. In nonfiction, they usually just sound wrong. Choose based on purpose, not habit.

The Takeaway

A double negative can either sink your credibility or sell your voice—it depends on whether you meant to use it.

In standard writing, avoid them. In creative writing, wield them with intent.

As with explosives, the key is control.

Try This

1. Fix the unintentional double negatives:
    - She didn't see nothing in the fog.
    - I can't hardly wait.
    - There isn't no way that's right.
2. Now, write two intentional double negatives that sound natural in dialogue or lyric style.
   (Example: "You ain't seen nothing yet.")
3. Bonus challenge: Rewrite a short sentence both ways—once correct, once stylistic—and note how tone changes.

Logical Leaps & Non Sequiturs (Grammar OK, Meaning... Not So Much)

Not every problem is a grammar problem. Some sentences are perfectly punctuated, beautifully balanced, and utterly nonsensical. That's when we've left the land of syntax and wandered into the swamps of logic.

STEP AWAY FROM THAT SENTENCE

A **non sequitur** (Latin for "it does not follow") is when one idea doesn't logically connect to the next—even if the grammar checks out. The result? Confused readers and an unintentional laugh track.

Instruction

Logical errors happen when sentence parts don't match in meaning or when a cause-and-effect relationship goes missing.

Examples:

No - She loved her cat because it was Tuesday. (Wait, what?)

No - Running late, the sandwich was eaten on the bus. (The sandwich wasn't running late—the *person* was.)

No - He said he'd call after dinner, but his phone died of exhaustion. (Figuratively clever, logically absurd.)

Common causes:

1. **Dangling logic**—modifiers or clauses attach to the wrong subject.
2. **Faulty comparisons**—comparing apples to metaphors.
    - **No** - The editor's desk is cleaner than the intern.
    - **Yes** - The editor's desk is cleaner than the intern's desk.
3. **Disconnected cause/effect**—when "because," "therefore," or "so" link ideas that don't actually relate.
    - **No** - She quit her job, so her hair grew back. (Interesting outcome, baffling cause.)

Fixing it:
Ask yourself:

- Does this sentence say what I mean?
- Do the parts logically connect?
- Would a reader stop and think, "Wait... what?"

If the answer to that last one is yes—rewrite.

The Takeaway

Grammar can make a sentence *correct*, but only logic can make it *clear*.

A technically perfect sentence that makes no sense is like a beautifully tuned violin playing nonsense notes.

Always test your sentences for sanity, not just structure. When your grammar and logic work together, readers glide through your meaning instead of tripping over it.

Try This

1. Spot and fix the logic fails:
    - The author finished her novel, so the weather improved.
    - Covered in icing, the baker admired the cake.
    - My dog is smarter than my homework.
2. Write one sentence that's grammatically correct but hilariously illogical—then rewrite it so it makes sense.
3. Bonus challenge: Take a paragraph of your own writing and look for cause-and-effect relationships. Are they truly connected, or just grammatically convenient?

Agreement and logic are where grammar stops being mechanical and starts being meaningful. You can have flawless punctuation and still confuse your reader if your ideas don't agree or connect.

When subjects and verbs match, pronouns find their partners, and logic keeps every clause tethered to sense, your writing feels trustworthy. Readers stop noticing the language and start absorbing the meaning.

Grammar isn't here to boss your sentences around; it's here to keep them from fighting. So let your words play nice—agree in number, stay consistent in thought, and never let a dangling idea wander off unsupervised.

Because clarity isn't just correctness. It's kindness.

Grammar Gremlins & Other Nightmares

You've survived nouns that refused to behave, verbs with time-travel issues, and adjectives drunk on adverbs. Congratulations. But before you hang up your editor's hat, beware: the gremlins are still out there.

These are the tiny, mean-spirited errors that slip through even the best drafts—the homonyms that haunt, the apostrophes that multiply in the dark, the modifiers that stalk the wrong noun like jealous exes. They're not dramatic enough to destroy a sentence, but they *will* make it twitch.

In this section, we'll hunt the usual suspects: the article arguments, the dangling dangers, the homonym havoc, and, of course, the apocalypse of misplaced apostrophes. Because polishing your writing isn't just about grandeur; it's about banishing the goblins hiding in your punctuation.

> The apostrophe didn't exist in English until the 1500s. Before that, everyone just guessed what belonged to whom—which explains medieval property disputes and family feuds.

Article Arguments (a/an/the/zero article choices)

Articles are small, sneaky words that decide how specific you're being—*a, an, the,* or nothing at all. They look harmless, but misuse them and your sentence either sounds like it came from a robot or from someone who's been living off-grid too long.

English articles are notoriously tricky because they deal in nuance, not logic. Knowing whether to use *a*, *an*, *the*, or nothing (the "zero article") depends less on rules and more on what you *mean*.

Instruction
1. Indefinite articles (*a, an*)
Use *a* or *an* for something general, non-specific, or mentioned for the first time.

- **Yes** - I saw **a** dragon. (one of many possible dragons)
- **Yes** - She wrote **an** essay. (any essay, not a particular one)

Use *a* before **consonant sounds** and *an* before **vowel sounds**. *(Note: it's about sound, not spelling.)*

- **Yes** - *A dragon* (starts with a consonant sound)
- **Yes** - *An apple* (starts with a vowel sound)

Heads-up on tricky sounds:
It's the **sound** that matters, not always the **letter**.

- Words like *unicorn* or *university* begin with the *"yoo"* sound—that's a **consonant sound**—so use *a*: **Yes** - *a unicorn, a university.*
- Words like *hour* or *honor* begin with a **silent h**, so they *start* with a vowel sound—use *an*: **Yes** - *an hour, an honor.*
If you're unsure, say it aloud. Your ear will usually tell you whether it flows or clunks.

2. Definite article (*the*)
Use *the* for something specific or already known to the reader.

- Yes - **The** dragon we met yesterday.
- Yes - She finished **the** essay she'd been writing.

Trickiest bits:

- Don't use *the* with generalizations: **No** - The happiness is important. **Yes** - Happiness is important.
- Don't skip *the* when you mean something specific: **No** - I closed window. **Yes** - I closed **the** window.

3. Zero article (no article)

Sometimes you don't need one at all—especially with general or abstract nouns, plural nouns, or proper names.

- **Yes** - Dragons love gold.
- **Yes** - Life is strange.
- **Yes** - Canada is cold.

The Takeaway

Articles are less about grammar and more about **focus**. They tell readers whether you're speaking broadly (*a dragon*) or specifically (*the dragon*).

Misusing them doesn't usually wreck a sentence—it just makes it sound off. Like a musician hitting the right note at the wrong time.

Get in the habit of asking:

- Am I talking about *any* one of these things, or *this* particular one? That question alone solves 90% of article confusion.

Try This

1. Fill in the correct article (or none):
    - ___ book on that shelf belongs to ___ student from

___ university in London.
- She wants to adopt ___ cat—not just any, but ___ one with one eye and attitude.
- ___ patience is a virtue, but not ___ one I possess.
2. Write three sentences using:
   - One with *a/an*
   - One with *the*
   - One with zero article
3. Bonus challenge: Take a paragraph of your own writing and remove every article. Read it aloud. Feel how robotic it sounds? Now add them back. That's the difference a few tiny words make.

> The article *the* is pronounced differently before vowels (*thee apple*) than consonants (*thuh dragon*), but most people never notice they do it.

Misplaced & Dangling Modifiers: The Stalker Edition

You've met these two before—the syntax creepers who can't take a hint.

A misplaced modifier attaches to the wrong noun; a dangling one attaches to no one at all.

They've already been arrested in the *Modifiers* chapter, but they keep breaking parole.

Example refresher:
No - *Covered in sprinkles, the baker admired the cake.*
Yes - *Covered in sprinkles, the cake gleamed as the baker admired it.*

Keep your modifiers close and your subjects closer. Otherwise, your sentences start sounding like tabloid headlines.

Homonym Havoc (there/their/they're; your/you're; affect/effect)

Homonyms are the shape-shifters of English—words that sound alike but mean entirely different things. They lurk in spellcheck-proof territory, waiting to embarrass even the most careful writer.

We've all been there: you hit "send," and only afterward notice you wrote *your amazing* instead of *you're amazing*. And you've just told them that *amazing* belongs to them—grammar-wise, that's true, but emotionally, it's a mess.

Homonym mix-ups aren't signs of ignorance; they're signs of typing too fast. But they can still make you look careless—and the Grammar Gremlins love that.

Instruction

Let's sort out the worst offenders:

There / Their / They're

- *There* = place or existence → There is the book.
- *Their* = possession → Their book is missing.
- *They're* = they are → They're reading that book.

Your / You're

- *Your* = possession → Your cat is judging me.
- *You're* = you are → You're absolutely right.

Its / It's

- *Its* = possession → The dragon lost its temper.
- *It's* = it is → It's dangerous to provoke a dragon.

Affect / Effect

- *Affect* = verb → The rain affected the crops.
- *Effect* = noun → The rain had a dramatic effect on the crops. (*Tip:* If you can replace it with *influence*, it's *affect*. If you can replace it with *result*, it's *effect*.)

Then / Than

- *Then* = time → Finish your tea, then we'll go.
- *Than* = comparison → Dragons are larger than donkeys.

The Takeaway

Homonyms are tiny saboteurs—they sneak past your brain because they sound right, not because they *are* right.

Slow down when you proofread. Spellcheck doesn't always catch words that are spelled correctly but used incorrectly.

When in doubt, say it aloud or test it in a full sentence. If your substitution changes the meaning, you've caught the gremlin.

Try This

1. Fix the homonym havoc:
   - Their going to regret loosing they're keys over there.
   - Your my favorite editor.
   - The potion had no visible affect.
   - Its going to rain, and the dragon will loose it's patience.
2. Write one short paragraph that correctly uses all these pairs.
3. Create a single, logically correct sentence that contains **there**, **their**, and **they're**—and still makes sense.

The Apostrophe Apocalypse (it's/its; plurals vs.

possessives)

If grammar had a doomsday scenario, it would be this: the apostrophe rising up to claim what was never its. Every day, signs fall, essays crumble, and otherwise decent sentences perish under the chaos of misplaced punctuation.

The apostrophe is meant for two things—**possession** and **contraction**—but it's been hijacked by every plural noun in sight. This is not a drill.

Instruction
It's / Its—The False Prophet of Possession

- *It's* = **it is** or **it has** → *It's raining. / It's been hours.*
- *Its* = **belongs to it** → *The dragon lost its temper.*
 Apostrophes never mark possession in *its*. Think of it as a pronoun like *his* or *hers*—no punctuation required.

Plural Catastrophes—The Horde of Random Apostrophes
No - Apple's for sale.
Yes - Apples for sale.
Apostrophes do **not** make words plural. Ever. If you're talking about more than one thing, just add *s* (or *es*) and walk away. The only exception is when plural letters or numbers might look confusing:
Yes - Mind your p's and q's.
Yes - She was born in the 1980s. (*No apostrophe needed unless it's possessive.*)

Possessive Collisions—Who Owns What?
To show ownership, add an apostrophe—carefully:

- Singular owner → **The dragon's hoard** (one dragon, one hoard)
- Plural owners → **The dragons' hoard** (many dragons, shared hoard)

STEP AWAY FROM THAT SENTENCE 147

- Irregular plural → **The children's stories**
  If you're ever unsure, rephrase with *of*: *the stories of the children*. If that works, you need an apostrophe.

Decades & Acronyms—The Riders of False Tradition
People still write *1980's music* or *FAQ's* thinking it's correct. It's not.
Yes - 1980s music.
Yes - FAQs.
Unless something belongs to that decade (*the 1980's influence*), no apostrophe is necessary.

The Takeaway
Apostrophes are punctuation, not decoration. Use them only when you're shortening words (*it's, don't, you're*) or showing ownership (*the dragon's treasure*).

Never use them for plurals, and never assume *it's* is possessive. If your sentence looks like it's hoarding apostrophes, it probably is.

Remember: every apostrophe must earn its place—or face grammatical exile.

Try This

1. Fix these apostrophe abominations:
   - The dragon's are restless.
   - Its a fine day for editing.
   - The 1990's were simpler times.
2. Write two sentences:
   - One showing singular possession.
   - One showing plural possession.
3. Create one sentence that includes *it's*, *its*, a plural noun, and a possessive noun—all correct. If your head doesn't hurt afterward, you've survived the Apocalypse.
4. Explain the difference: The authors' conference is next week vs. The author's conference is next week.

You've made it through many of the challenges that grammar has to offer—from runaway modifiers to rogue apostrophes. Congratulations. You've survived the Grammar Gremlins.

But here's the twist ending: you'll still break the rules sometimes. And that's okay.

Because grammar isn't a prison; it's a toolkit. The point of learning the rules isn't to live in fear of them—it's to know when and how to break them with purpose. Once you understand *why* something works, you can bend it, twist it, or toss it out entirely to create voice, rhythm, or impact.

The real mastery of grammar is confidence—the ability to write boldly, edit ruthlessly, and trust your ear when your instinct says, *Yes, this works.*

So go ahead. Start a sentence with *and*. End one with a preposition. Split an infinitive like a rebel poet. Just know exactly what you're doing when you do it.

Because grammar isn't about perfection. It's about control.

Breaking the Rules on Purpose

You've learned the rules. You've wrestled the commas, negotiated peace treaties between verbs and subjects, and sent rogue modifiers packing. Now comes the best part: learning how to break the rules *intelligently*.

Every writer with style eventually does. The difference between a mistake and a masterpiece is intent.

Instruction

The rules of grammar exist for one reason—clarity. Once you understand how they work, you can bend them to create rhythm, voice, humor, and mood.

When to Break Them (and Why):

- **For voice**—Real people don't speak in perfect syntax. Dialogue and personal essays thrive on fragments, contractions, and deliberate slang.
  Yes - *Wasn't ready. Didn't care.*
- **For emphasis**—A short, rule-breaking sentence after a long one can jolt the reader awake.
  Yes - *And then it stopped.*
- **For rhythm**—Sometimes a technically "incorrect" structure *sounds* better because it flows naturally. Trust your ear.
  Yes - *To boldly go where no one has gone before.* (Yes, that split infinitive was worth it.)
- **For authenticity**—Rule-breaking can capture tone, era, or character. A stiffly "perfect" sentence often sounds artificial.

But don't break rules out of laziness. Break them like an artist who knows exactly what will happen when the brush hits the canvas.

The Takeaway

Grammar is freedom disguised as structure. The better you understand it, the more confidently you can shape it to your will.

Breaking the rules on purpose isn't rebellion; it's mastery. It's what separates a sloppy writer from a stylist.

Remember: you can't bend what you don't first understand. So learn the rules, love them, then occasionally wink at them and step over the line.

Try This

1. Write one paragraph that obeys every grammar rule you know.
2. Rewrite it breaking at least three of them *on purpose*—for rhythm, tone, or emotional punch.
3. Compare the two. Which version feels more alive?
4. Bonus challenge: Identify a "rule" you were once afraid to break. Then, write a sentence that shatters it spectacularly—and still works.

Grammar isn't a cage; it's choreography. Once you know the steps, you can dance however you like.

Now go make some beautiful, deliberate mistakes.

Author's Note

If you made it this far, congratulations—you've officially survived grammar boot camp without losing your mind (or your Oxford commas).

Writing this book was a joy, a challenge, and occasionally a staring contest with the English language itself. If you've ever found yourself arguing with a comma, consoling a dangling modifier, or whispering "what even *is* subjunctive mood?" into the void—you're in good company.

Grammar isn't about perfection. It's about *possibility*. Once you stop fearing it, you realize it's just another creative tool—one that helps your meaning land exactly where you want it to.

Thank you for walking this line between logic and language with me. Thank you for laughing at the rules, questioning them, and learning how to wield them instead of obeying them.

And thank you, most of all, for caring enough about words to make them better.

Now go write something worth breaking a few rules for.

— *Saoirse Temple*

Glossary of Terms, Tricks, and Tiny Tyrants

In case you ever forget what a gerund is—or just enjoy watching definitions misbehave—here's a crash course through the creatures that haunt English grammar. Some are useful, some are sneaky, and some will ruin your day if left unattended. Handle with care, preferably while holding a red pen.

A

Active Voice—When the subject performs the action rather than receives it.

Example: *Saoirse edited the manuscript.*

Unofficial definition: Grammar's extrovert—it knows who did it and isn't afraid to say so.

Adjective—A word that describes a noun or pronoun.

Example: purple, sleepy, ill-advised.

Unofficial definition: A noun's favorite accessory—the glitter it wears to get noticed.

Adverb—A word that describes a verb, adjective, or another adverb, often ending in *-ly*.

Example: quietly, recklessly, occasionally truthfully.

Unofficial definition: The overachiever of grammar—never content to leave anything unmodified.

Antecedent—The word a pronoun refers to.

Example: Saoirse wrote a book, and she loved it. ("Saoirse" is the antecedent of "she.")

Antonym—A word with the opposite meaning of another.

Example: hot/cold; love/hate.

Unofficial definition: The word that ruins your attempt at optimism.

STEP AWAY FROM THAT SENTENCE

Apostrophe—A punctuation mark used for possession (*the dragon's treasure*) or contraction (*it's raining*).

Unofficial definition: The punctuation equivalent of a cat—does exactly what it wants, when it wants, and dares you to stop it.

Appositive—A noun or phrase that renames another noun beside it.

Example: My dragon, Steve, loves gold.

Unofficial definition: The sentence's name tag: "Hi, I'm explaining that thing you just met."

Article—The tiny word before a noun that signals specificity or generality: *a, an, the.*

Unofficial definition: The smallest words with the biggest identity issues.

C

Clause—A group of words with a subject and verb. Can be independent (a full sentence) or dependent (needs backup).

Unofficial definition: Grammar's power couple—one does the action, the other completes the thought.

Comma—A small pause that can change everything.

Example: Let's eat, Grandma vs. *Let's eat Grandma.*

Unofficial definition: The difference between dinner and being dinner.

Comma Splice—The tragic love story between two sentences joined only by a comma.

Unofficial definition: Proof that punctuation and commitment don't mix well.

Conjunction—A connector word that joins ideas: *and, but, or, so, because.*

Unofficial definition: The social butterfly of grammar—can't stand when words aren't mingling.

Contraction—A shortened form of two words, joined by an apostrophe.

Example: don't, can't, it's.

Unofficial definition: Grammar's lazy genius—does less work, sounds more natural.

Correlative Conjunctions—Paired conjunctions that work together: *either/or, neither/nor, both/and, not only/but also.*

Unofficial definition: Grammar's power couples. Occasionally codependent.

D

Dangling Modifier—A descriptive phrase with no clear subject to attach to.

Example: Walking down the street, the rain soaked my coat.

Unofficial definition: A sentence that's gone out without a chaperone.

Dependent Clause—A clause that can't stand alone.

Example: Because I said so.

Unofficial definition: The needy friend who always requires context.

Direct Object—The noun or pronoun that receives the action of a verb.

Example: She threw the book. ("book" is the direct object.)

E

Ellipsis—Three dots indicating an omission or pause in thought.

Example: And then... everything changed.

Unofficial definition: The punctuation mark that lives for drama.

G

Gerund—A verb that's moonlighting as a noun, ending in *-ing.*

Example: Running is exhausting.

Unofficial definition: The overworked part of speech that's doing too much.

Grammar—The structure that keeps meaning from collapsing.

Unofficial definition: The art of making words behave—just enough to set them free again.

H

Homonym—A word that sounds like another word but has a different meaning.
Example: to, too, two.
Unofficial definition: The reason English teachers drink.

I

Independent Clause—A clause that can stand alone as a complete sentence.
Example: The dragon snored.
Unofficial definition: The free spirit of grammar—doesn't need anyone to complete it.
Indirect Object—The person or thing that benefits from the verb's action.
Example: She threw him the book. ("him" is the indirect object.)
Infinitive—The base form of a verb, often introduced by *to*.
Example: to write, to sleep, to procrastinate.
Interjection—A short exclamation that expresses emotion.
Example: Wow! Oops! Hey!
Unofficial definition: Grammar's jump scare.

M

Metaphor—A comparison that says one thing *is* another.
Example: Her mind was a storm.
Unofficial definition: A lie we all agree to believe because it's prettier that way.
Modifier—Any word or phrase that adds detail.
Unofficial definition: The decorator of grammar—sometimes tasteful, sometimes "too much throw pillow."
Mood (Indicative, Imperative, Subjunctive)—The tone of the verb that shows intention or attitude.
Example: Write the book. (imperative) / *If I were a dragon...* (subjunctive)
Unofficial definition: How your verbs feel about what's happening.

N

Noun—A person, place, thing, or idea.
Example: writer, dragon, grammar, chaos.
Unofficial definition: The building blocks of meaning. Without nouns, you've got... nothing.

O

Oxymoron—Two contradictory words paired together.
Example: jumbo shrimp, deafening silence.
Unofficial definition: When English can't make up its mind.

P

Parallelism—Using the same grammatical structure for related ideas.
Example: She likes reading, writing, and editing.
Unofficial definition: Grammar's choreographer—insists everyone hits the same beat.

Participle—A verb form acting as an adjective.
Example: the broken typewriter, the glowing moon.

Passive Voice—When the subject receives the action rather than performs it.
Example: The manuscript was edited by Saoirse.
Unofficial definition: Grammar's introvert—something happens, but no one wants to take credit.

Phrase—A group of words that acts as a single unit but lacks both subject and verb.
Example: under the table, after the storm, in theory.

Predicate—The part of a sentence that tells what the subject does or is.
Example: In *The dragon sleeps,* "sleeps" is the predicate.

Preposition—A word that shows relationship, usually in time, space, or direction.
Example: on, in, under, beside, during.
Unofficial definition: The sentence's GPS—constantly shouting "recalculating."

Pronoun—A word that stands in for a noun.

Example: he, she, they, it, who.

Unofficial definition: The understudy who shows up when the star noun needs a break.

Pronoun-Antecedent Agreement—When a pronoun matches its original noun in number and gender.

Example: Each writer must find their voice.

R

Run-On Sentence—When multiple independent clauses collide without proper punctuation or conjunctions.

Unofficial definition: The marathon of grammar—no breath, no breaks, no survivors.

S

Semicolon—The halfway house between a comma and a period.

Unofficial definition: The punctuation mark that screams, "I know what I'm doing."

Sentence Fragment—A clause missing a key piece—subject, verb, or complete thought.

Example: If only I had known.

Unofficial definition: The cliffhanger of grammar.

Simile—A comparison using *like* or *as.*

Example: Her laughter was like thunder.

Unofficial definition: A metaphor that wants to make sure no one takes it too literally.

Split Infinitive—When an adverb wedges itself inside an infinitive.

Example: to boldly go.

Unofficial definition: The grammatical scandal that launched a thousand Star Trek quotes.

Subject-Verb Agreement—The grammatical handshake that keeps sentences civil.

Unofficial definition: When one side drops the handshake, everything feels awkward.

Synonym—A word with the same or nearly the same meaning as another.

Example: happy/joyful; begin/start.

Unofficial definition: A linguistic doppelgänger—looks innocent until it slightly changes the nuance.

Syntax—The arrangement of words and phrases to form sentences.

Unofficial definition: Grammar's architecture—the blueprint for making meaning sound beautiful.

T

Tense—The verb form that shows time.

Example: past, present, future.

Unofficial definition: Proof that writers are always either regretting, narrating, or planning something.

V

Verb—A word that expresses action or being.

Example: run, dream, become, is.

Unofficial definition: The engine of language—without it, the sentence just sits there, quietly existing and achieving nothing.

Voice (Active/Passive)—Indicates whether the subject performs the action (*active*) or receives it (*passive*).

Example: The editor fixed the sentence vs. *The sentence was fixed by the editor.*

About the Author

Saoirse Temple is a professional editor and book coach who specializes in helping indie authors make their dream of being published come true. A long-time advocate of self-publishing, Saoirse enjoys sharing in the success of authors of all types of works. When she isn't editing or writing, she spends her time knitting, cross stitching, and exploring Grande Prairie, where she makes her home. Follow Saoirse on Facebook: www.facebook.com/saoirsetempleediting Patreon: www.patreon.com/SaoirseTemple Instagram: @saoirsealt

Read more at www.saoirsetemple.com.

www.ingramcontent.com/pod-product-compliance
Lightning Source LLC
LaVergne TN
LVHW011912080426
835508LV00007BA/502